D1570871

THE TRIUMPH OF CORPORATE CAPITALISM
IN FRANCE, 1867-1914

THE TRIUMPH OF
CORPORATE CAPITALISM
IN FRANCE
1867-1914

CHARLES E. FREEDEMAN

UNIVERSITY OF ROCHESTER PRESS

Copyright © The Estate of Charles E. Freedeman 1993

All Rights Reserved. Except as permitted under current legislation
no part of this work may be photocopied, stored in a retrieval system,
published, performed in public, adapted, broadcast,
transmitted, recorded or reproduced in any form or by any means,
without the prior permission of the copyright owner

First published 1993

University of Rochester Press
200 Administration Building, University of Rochester
Rochester, New York 14627, USA
and at PO Box 9, Woodbridge, Suffolk IP12 3DF, UK

ISBN 1 878822 22 5

Library of Congress Cataloging-in-Publication Data
Freedeman, Charles Eldon, 1926–
  The triumph of corporate capitalism in France, 1867–1914 /
Charles E. Freedeman.
    p. cm.
  A chronological sequel to the author's Joint stock enterprise in
France 1807–1867.
  Includes bibliographical references and index.
  ISBN 1–878822–22–5
  1. Corporations – France – History. 2. Corporations – France –
Finance – History. I. Freedeman, Charles Eldon, 1926– Joint-
stock enterprise in France, 1807–1867. II. Title.
HD2855.F74   1993
338.7'4'0944–dc20   93–1897

British Library Cataloguing-in-Publication Data
Freedeman, Charles E.
    Triumph of Corporate Capitalism in
    France, 1867–1914
    I. Title
    330.120944
    ISBN 1–878822–22–5

This publication is printed on acid-free paper

Printed in the United States of America

TABLE OF CONTENTS

TABLES AND GRAPHS

ABBREVIATIONS USED IN THE TEXT

CPA   *Société en Commandite par actions*
MF   million francs
SA   *Société anonyme*
SARL   *Société à résponsabilité limitée*

PREFACE

In an earlier book, *Joint-Stock Enterprise in France, 1807-1867: From Privileged Company to Modern Corporation* (Chapel Hill: University of North Carolina Press, 1979), Charles Freedeman traced the evolution of the corporate form of business organization in France from the napoleonic *Code de Commerce* of 1807 to the advent of "free" incorporation: the law of 1867 that enabled businesses to assume the corporate form (in French, that of a *société anonyme*) without specific government authorization. That book was widely praised, even by French scholars — a rarity for books on French subjects by American authors — and is now regarded as the definitive work on its subject.

The present volume is the logical and chronological sequel to the earlier one. It describes the exfoliation of the corporate form of organization from the law of 1867 to the outbreak of war in 1914, and details the debates over the attempts to "reform" that law, both by making it more restrictive and more liberal. But it does more than that; it considers the controversies over the role of foreign investment in the French economy, the structure of the banking system and its role in domestic industrial finance, and the growth of industrial concentration. Those chapters, III and IV, are in my opinion, the most valuable contribution of the book.

Throughout the nineteenth century, especially in its latter half, citizens of France invested abroad, at first in its neighbors (Spain, Portugal, Italy, Belgium, Switzerland, western Germany), subsequently farther afield (notably the Ottoman Empire and Egypt) and overseas. After the Franco-Russian alliance of 1894 French investors, with the active encouragement of their government (and even before, without such encouragement), invested huge sums in both public and private Russian securities — to their sorrow when the Bolshevik government of V. I. Lenin repudiated all debts, public and private, incurred under the tsarist regime. In 1914 French foreign investments amounted to more than 50 billion francs (about $10 billion), second only to the British. In the beginning, resources for the investments were provided by a large export surplus in commodity trade, but from the 1870s earnings on previous investments more than sufficed to finance the new investments.

Before 1848 the investments were facilitated by private French banks, especially the members of *la haute banque parisienne*, but in the 1850s and

1860s these were joined by large joint-stock banks, such as the Crédit Mobilier, the Comptoir d'Escompte, the Crédit Lyonnais, and the Société Générale. After the law of 1867 on *sociétés anonymes* the number of joint-stock banks accelerated, as did the flow of foreign investments. Some contemporary observers as well as subsequent historians saw a link between those trends, and accused the banks of exporting capital at the expense of French domestic industry. Freedeman had no difficulty in showing the speciousness of those arguments.

A similar, related criticism of the joint-stock banks accused them of neglecting French domestic industry in favor of their foreign interests. It is true that there was a tradition in some French industries or industrial firms of *autofinancement*, of self-finance by means of re-invested profits. What was not clear in the literature on the subject was whether this policy was freely chosen by the firms in question, or whether it was forced on them by deliberate neglect by the banks. Freedeman shows by a number of case studies based on archival sources that in many instances the policy of self-finance was freely chosen, and that in others firms had no difficulty in raising funds either from the banks directly or through the capital market with bank assistance. On the whole, the capital market, of which the banks were a part, functioned rather efficiently.[1]

Finally, in Chapter V, Freedeman considers whether the law of 1867 facilitated or hindered competition and the growth of industrial concentration. As in all industrial nations, there was a pronounced tendency for French industrial firms to grow in size in the decades before World War I. This did not necessarily result, however, in a lessening of competition. New firms — small, medium and large — making use of the corporate form of organization entered most industries. Unlike the case of the United States, where the Sherman Antitrust Act stimulated the growth of huge corporations like the United States Steel Company, or that of Germany, where the law explicitly allowed the formation of cartels, the law in France was less explicit, more ambiguous. Cartels existed, as Freedeman shows (contrary to the opinion of some scholars); but they did so in muted form, without arousing adverse public opinion. All of these considerations lead Freedeman to his final conclusion: corporate capitalism existed and flourished in France.

Freedeman devoted more than ten years to this book, in archives and libraries, in France and the United States. He was a careful, deliberate scholar. He presented his findings in clear and measured prose, accessible to

---

[1] Further information on both these subjects — foreign investment and industrial finance — may be found in a recent book that Freedeman did not have the opportunity to consult: Rondo Cameron and V. I. Bovykin, eds., *International Banking, 1870-1914* (New York: Oxford University Press, 1991). Three of the authors are French.

any interested, intelligent reader. The manuscript was substantially complete by the spring of 1991, when the author was diagnosed as suffering from lung cancer and given less than a year to live. He spent much of the following months putting the finishing touches on the manuscript, preparing it for publication, but he died before he could submit it to a publisher. The University of Rochester Press deserves the appreciation of the world of scholarship for making the book available to the larger audience that it merits.

Rondo Cameron
Emory University

INTRODUCTION

En fait, les grandes sociétés par actions sont en train de modifier profondément notre régime économique, notre système de propriété, notre moralité, notre droit

Adolphe Coste, 1892

The development of the modern business corporation may be divided into three stages. The first stage saw the creation of the privileged trading companies of the 17th and 18th centuries for which the state itself often acted as the promoter. These state-chartered enterprises generally enjoyed exclusive privileges, which came under attack at the end of the 18th century. From the beginning, the corporation was developed to provide large amounts of capital for an enterprise, which was normally beyond the capacity of single, or a few, individuals. Until the end of the 18th century overseas trading companies constituted the prototype of joint-stock companies.

But with the coming of first canals and then railroads, and the emergence of large-scale industrial enterprises requiring huge sums of capital, the joint-stock form of business organization was adapted, out of necessity, for their use. During this second stage, encompassing the first two-thirds of the 19th century, incorporation was liberalized, but the government either retained the right explicitly to authorize each corporation, or denied, as in England, their owners the protection of limited liability. These restrictions generated pressures for free incorporation with limited liability. During this period the corporation acquired a measure of public legitimacy, but where the authorization of a corporation required governmental approval, charges of favoritism and corruption lingered. Bowing to growing economic and political pressures, most western countries in the 1860s and 1870s adopted legislation permitting free incorporation with limited liability, though subject to restrictions deemed necessary to protect stockholders and the general public. This marked the beginning of a third stage in the history of the modern corporation, which is still with us.

This book is a continuation of my *Joint-Stock Enterprise in France, 1807-1867, From Privileged Company to Modern Corporation* (Chapel Hill, 1979), which traced the history of the corporate form of business organization in France from the elaboration of the *Code de Commerce* of 1807 to the law of 1867 that freed the corporation from the necessity of government authorization. By 1867 the corporation assumed its definitive form with regard to structure, operation and governance which was to change little thereafter. Although there were variations between the corporations of France and those of Britain and elsewhere, mostly involving the degree of restrictions governing their formation and operation, their basic structure was not dissimilar. This was partly because the international capitalist system exerted pressure for a degree of uniformity; also, to a considerable extent, the corporate law of other continental European countries followed the French model.

Freed from the necessity for government authorization after 1867, the number of corporations rapidly expanded. Chapter I deals with the numbers and capitalization of new incorporations, and with the relative decline of an alternative form of corporation, the *société en commandite par actions*. Into what sectors did the corporation expand? One innovation of the period was the use of the corporate form of business organization by medium-size family firms, which organized "private" corporations that did not issue shares to the public. Finally, the question of how did the formation of corporations in France compare with that of Great Britain and of Germany. Did France lag in the use of this quintessential instrument of modern capitalism?

The debate over corporate law did not end with the law of 1867, Chapter II deals with the continuing controversy over corporate law, particularly over the degree of restrictiveness and the scope of safeguards that were necessary to protect the public and shareholders against fraudulent promotion of corporations. In this debate two groups confronted one another: On the one side were those who would stringently regulate the formation and operation of corporations, and increasingly cited German law as the example to be followed. On the other side were those who would liberalize the law of 1867, and held up the examples of Great Britain and of Belgium as worthy of emulation. Depressions and financial scandals influenced the ebb and flow of restrictionist sentiment.

Another contemporary debate, which has continued to the present, involves the transformation of the banking system attendant on the rise of gigantic corporate banks. It was alleged that these banks channelled French savings abroad to the detriment of French domestic industry. In the view of some, French corporations were "starved for capital" while billions were invested abroad, particularly in foreign government bonds. Chapter III explores the genesis of this controversy and in the attempt to provide some answers to the questions that it raised, discusses the role of banks in financing domestic industry. This role was much more positive than the critics assert.

In addition to support, or lack thereof, from banks, what other financing options were available for industrial corporations? This is the subject of Chapter IV, which analyses the experience of a score of corporations drawn from different sectors of the economy. The evidence suggests that the alleged forced reliance of French industry on self-financing is a myth.

Chapter V examines the impact of increasing numbers and size of corporations on the economy. The rise of the corporation threatened the competitive economic model of classical liberalism. In the last two decades of the 19th century, in France and elsewhere, corporations increasingly sought to escape from the rigors of competition by whatever means open to them. In France, the courts, government officials and the public adopted an increasingly benign attitude toward the spread of cartels, particularly toward those which exercised their power with moderation.

In the years between 1867 and 1914, the triumph of the corporation created a new and different kind of capitalism than that which characterized earlier phases of capitalist development. It is generally recognized that the dominant merchant capitalism of the 17th and 18th centuries was succeeded by the industrial capitalism of the 19th century, and that toward the end of the 19th century a new phase arrived, variously dubbed as "monopoly capitalism" or "finance capitalism." "Corporate capitalism" is a more accurate label to denote the phase in which we still find ourselves.

CHAPTER I

THE AGE OF THE CORPORATION

. . . l'initiative individuelle a acquis plus de confiance et de maturité; l'intervention de la puissance publique dans les rapports entre particuliers a paru chaque jour moins utile.

Exposé des motifs, projet de loi sur les sociétés, 1865

The Business Corporation in 1867[1]

In 1867, the French legislature inaugurated a new era in the history of the corporation by repealing the requirement in the Commercial Code of 1807 that subjected the founding of a corporation (*société anonyme*) to the consent of the government. During the intervening sixty year period between the promulgation of the Commercial Code and the enactment of the law of 1867, obtaining authorization for a *société anonyme* (SA) involved a long and arduous process of review by the ministries of commerce or public works and by the Conseil d'Etat that, under normal circumstances, required six months to a year. In addition to the statutory requirements of the Commercial Code of 1807, the enterprise had to conform to rules laid down by the Conseil d'Etat, a body that, in fact, made the final decision with regard to authorization. The "administrative jurisprudence" of the Conseil d'Etat governing the formation of corporations emerged gradually in the early years of the century and by the 1830s it assumed a fixed form that was to change little down to 1867. The Conseil d'Etat tried consistently, but not always successfully, to reserve the SA for large enterprises of "public utility." Only a few small enterprises, mostly in the provinces, succeeded in gaining authorization. The Conseil demanded that the nominal value of

---

[1] The material in this section is mostly drawn from Charles Freedeman, *Joint-Stock Enterprise in France, 1807-1867: From Privileged Company to Modern Corporation* (Chapel Hill, 1979).

1

shares be at least 500 francs, that all the capital of the enterprise be subscribed in advance, and that at least one-quarter had to be paid in. None of these requirements were to be found in the Commercial Code, but were added at the discretion of the Conseil, as were regulations mandating the constitution of a reserve fund and provisions determining voting in shareholders' meetings. If the Conseil deemed that the enterprise's working capital was inadequate, it would not be authorized unless it agreed to raise the capital to a figure the Conseil determined was acceptable. Projected corporations had to include these and a myriad of other requirements in their by-laws in order to receive authorization. Although the Conseil d'Etat played a leading role in shaping the SA, other groups contributed, directly or indirectly: the ministries, especially commerce and public works, legislators, notaries, judges, professors, investors and even businessmen.

As a result of the restrictions placed upon the formation of SAs, only 642 were formed between 1807 and 1867,[2] an average of less than 11 per year, but they included most of the largest joint-stock companies created in France. The number of SAs authorized in any given year reflected the business cycle, though there was a tendency for the number of incorporations to increase over time. During the last 15 years of government authorization (1852-1867), the formation of SAs averaged almost 15 per year. The authorization procedure offered no guarantee of final success as the discretionary authority of the ministries and the Conseil d'Etat was absolute. Certain types of enterprise were simply ruled out, such as retail enterprises and, until the 1850s, banks. Only about one in ten applications for authorization by banks were successful, and the successful ones normally possessed some political clout. Although the rate of success was higher for other types of enterprises, many aspiring corporations failed to receive authorization, and many more, discouraged by the authorization gauntlet, renounced the attempt. For enterprises that were denied authorization, or declined to apply, there existed a serviceable corporate substitute, the *société en commandite par actions*, an original French invention (in its 19th century form), which was borrowed by other continental European countries, though not by Great Britain and the United States.

The *société en commandite par actions* (CPA) was a cross between the corporate and partnership forms of business organization. It was run by a manager (*gérant*), who was virtually omnipotent and subject to unlimited liability. The shareholders resembled silent partners in a partnership, who provided capital and enjoyed limited liability, but they possessed no voice in

---

[2] In a recent definitive study on the legal aspects of the SA between 1807 and 1867, Anne Lefebvre-Teillard has counted 651 SAs. The main divergence involves her inclusion of ten semi-official comptoirs d'escompte created in 1848 and subsequently transformed into private companies. *La Société anonyme au XIX siècle* (Paris, 1985), pp. 64-65.

2

management. Unlike the shareholders of an SA, who, at least theoretically, could choose and dismiss members of the board of directors, the shareholders of a CPA had no authority over the *gérant*. This form of business organization managed to slip into the *Code de Commerce* almost by accident. It was absent from earlier drafts of the *Code*, but the protest of port cities, which employed a *commenda*-type organization for the outfitting of ships, caused it to be included, though not without some misgivings. Although not intended to serve as a corporate substitute, the CPA was pressed into that role when the Conseil d'Etat decided to enforce a restrictive policy in granting authorization for SAs.

Only small numbers of CPAs appeared until the mid-1820s, but between 1826 and 1835 the number normally ranged from 100 to 150 per year. They enjoyed greater popularity in Paris than in the provinces, the Paris area accounting for a majority of all CPAs founded. The year 1836 marked the beginning of a speculative boom and the CPA was its chosen instrument. In 1837, registration of CPAs climbed to over 400, of which 287 with a total nominal capital of over 500 million francs (hereafter MF), were in the Paris area (the realized capital was much less, probably between one-fifth and one-third the nominal figure). Another 301 CPAs with a nominal capital of 800 MF were founded in the Paris area during the first seven months of 1838. Many, perhaps half, of the CPAs formed during the speculative boom were founded by promoters without substance, who were often more interested in fleecing a gullible public than founding serious enterprises.

The government moved to end the speculative boom and the fraudulent creation of CPAs by introducing a bill in the Chamber in 1838 that would eliminate the CPA completely. The Chamber's committee wanted a less drastic course of action, proposing instead heavy restrictions on the creation of CPAs rather than their complete elimination. Though it appeared that some restrictive legislation would be passed, neither bill came before the Chamber in 1838 owing to political rivalries that had nothing to do with the CPAs. By the following year, the collapse of the boom made the reform seem less urgent, and the CPA received a reprieve until 1856, when in the midst of a similar speculative boom, restrictive legislation was passed that effectively killed the CPA as a promotional vehicle for large enterprise. But during its heyday between 1836 and 1856, approximately 4,500 CPAs were formed, an average of over 200 per year. Although many were still-born, and many endured for only a short time, and others were simply schemes for unscrupulous promoters to defraud the public, the CPA was widely used for all types of enterprise, and was especially important for banking, insurance, transport, metallurgy, manufacturing, and publishing companies. Because of the difficulty in obtaining authorization for an SA, the CPA provided entrepreneurs with a viable alternative, which made a significant contribution to French economic development. Although accurate figures

3

are lacking on the realized capital of these enterprises, it is probable that the capital of the CPAs during the period 1836-1856 was at least as large as the approximately 2.8 billion francs accounted for by SAs for the same period.

With the existence of the CPA as a vehicle for both large and small enterprise until 1856, the development of the French economy was not hampered unduly by the restrictions surrounding the formation of SAs. In fact, until 1856 French legislation was more liberal than any in Europe and provided a model for continental emulation. Even the British felt the attraction in the early 1850s when sentiment existed to import the CPA from France in order to secure the protection of limited liability for shareholders, which English law did not afford.[3] A number of English firms with majority, or wholly, English capital and management, and operating in England, were founded in Paris as CPAs. But the CPA, which retained unlimited liability for the managers of the enterprise and gave them almost dictatorial control, could be regarded as only a convenient substitute for the corporation that combined both free incorporation and limited liability for all and, unlike the CPA, gave the stockholders *de jure* control of the enterprise. In the end the English declined to import the CPA. Instead, the liberal English Limited Liability Act of 1856 led the way by granting the right of limited liability to all comers.

The breakthrough in England occurred in the same year the French legislature, reacting to a speculative boom that saw the creation of numerous fraudulent CPAs, placed numerous restrictions on their creation.[4] This restrictive legislation, which drastically reduced the founding of CPAs, triggered a campaign for liberalization in France, a campaign that was aided by the negotiation of a series of bilateral commercial treaties which recognized the right of foreign enterprises to operate freely in France. The treaty with Belgium, which came into effect in 1857, and the treaty with Great Britain (1862) were particularly important as both countries now possessed more liberal laws than France governing the creation of joint-stock companies. It was also argued that the movement toward freer trade, inaugurated in 1860, made imperative the liberalization of French law so that her businessmen would not be at a competitive disadvantage. The government agreed, and sponsored legislation domesticating the English limited liability company in France, even to the extent of adopting the name *société à responsabilité limitée* (SARL). But the French version of the limited liability company, as its critics tirelessly pointed out, was less liberal than that across the channel.

---

[3]   Under the Joint-Stock Company Act of 1844, a corporation could be freely formed in England, but stockholders were subject to unlimited liability.

[4]   For a discussion of the provisions of the 1856 law, see Freedeman, *Joint-Stock Enterprise*, pp. 108-113.

The law of 1863 limited the maximum capital of the SARL to 20 MF and imposed numerous restrictions on the freedom of promoters.[5]

The clamor for liberalization did not abate with the creation of the SARL. Little more than a year later, the government agreed that the time had come to release the SA from the necessity of obtaining government authorization. Even within the administration, some came to see the advantage in relieving the government of the inconvenience of appearing to guarantee the future prospects of an enterprise through the conferring of authorization. Free incorporation would also permit the government to avoid the imputation that favoritism affected the granting of corporate charters. Undeniably, the system of authorization tended to favor old established interests, unless they were politically out of favor. Including an influential personnage (*e.g.*, the Duc de Morny) among the promoters helped to smooth the passage to authorization. The projected law would end the system of authorization. The new law, whose enactment was delayed until 1867, provided a fundamental charter for French corporate enterprise that was to endure for the next one hundred years.

Although it ended government authorization, the law provided a mandated general structure for the SA that closely resembled the form that had been shaped over the previous sixty years under the auspices of the Conseil d'Etat.[6] Instead of the intervention of the government in each case, the law, and interested parties, would now perform insofar as possible the role of the Conseil d'Etat. All the capital of the enterprise had to be subscribed and at least one-quarter had to be paid-in (one-half if the enterprise were to issue bearer shares, *actions au porteur*). The minimum value of shares was 500 francs for companies capitalized at over 200,000 francs and 100 francs for companies whose nominal capital was less than 200,000 francs. The company could not be definitively founded until the subscribers of shares had an opportunity to review and formally pass upon the company's by-laws, and particularly to consider the valuation of any real assets that were being exchanged for shares or cash in the new company. This provision was an attempt to eliminate a major source of fraud in the pre-1856 CPA when promoters created companies to unload overvalued to worthless assets on unsuspecting shareholders. The form of governance of the enterprise (stockholders' meetings and a board of directors) was mandated, as were the periodic issuance of financial statements. If three-fourths of the capital were lost, the question of dissolution had to be posed to the shareholders. The new law mandated a reserve fund equal to 10% of the enterprise's capital, to

---

[5] Ibid., pp. 136-38. During the four year period that the law was in force, 338 SARLs were founded, almost equally distributed between Paris and the rest of France, an average of 84 per year.

[6] Government authorization was retained for life insurance companies until 1905.

be raised by an annual levy of 5% on profits. Having provided what were thought to be adequate safeguards for their founding and operation, SAs were now allowed unfettered access to the economic jungle. With the end of government authorization for the formation of the SA, the SARL, no longer deemed of use, was discontinued.

Confining the SA to the traditional mold drew criticism at the time from both inside and outside the Corps Legislatif by those who would establish an almost complete freedom for promoters to do as they wished, subject only to adequate disclosure. Emile Ollivier, who introduced a bill along these lines as an alternative to the government's bill, and Joseph Garnier, the influential editor of the *Journal des économistes*, were the chief advocates of this course. Although Ollivier's bill managed to muster almost a quarter of the votes in the Corps Legislatif, the times, as Garnier recognized, were un-propitious,[7] though similar proposals were to re-emerge periodically until the end of the century. In spite of its restrictions, the new law did confer certain undeniable advantages. Promoters could now avoid inordinate delays in founding a corporation; small enterprises, discriminated against by the Conseil d'Etat, could now utilize the SA form, avoiding the inconveniences of the partnership or CPA forms of organization. And on innumerable counts (*e.g.*, the amount of the enterprise's working capital and provisions for borrowing) promoters no longer had to follow the dictates of the ministry or the Conseil d'Etat, as it was impossible for the law to provide for all contingencies. The rapid rise in the number of new SAs in the 15 years following the law is ample testimony to the restrictiveness of the old system. From an average of almost 15 per year during the period 1852-1867, the number rose to an annual average of 362 for the period 1868-1882.

Although there are reasonably accurate figures on the formation of joint-stock companies, we do not have accurate information on their mortality. The number of joint-stock enterprises existing in 1867, their total capitalization, and the relation of their numbers and capitalization to traditional forms of enterprise (partnerships and proprietorships) cannot be stated with accuracy. Three different types of joint-stock enterprises existed in 1867: SAs, CPAs, and SARLs. Of the 642 SAs authorized by the government between 1807 and 1867, probably only 200 were alive and operating in 1867; and about one-half of these were listed on the Paris Bourse. Of the casualties, most wound up with losses to shareholders, a few suffered bankruptcy leaving unsatisfied liabilities, many were merged with other SAs, sometimes forming new ones, and a few reached their term (the Conseil d'Etat insisted upon a time limit of 99 years or less) and were re-authorized, or, in rare instances, were denied re-authorization.

---

[7]   *Moniteur universel*, 28 May 1867, p. 640 and 29 May 1867, pp. 643ff. For the text and discussion of Ollivier's bill; *Journal des économistes*, 2nd ser. (1865), pp. 310-21.

If, as some contemporaries believed, the mortality rate among SAs was high (it probably was not, but that raises the question of norms), it was much higher for the approximately 7,100 CPAs registered during the same period, mostly between 1836 and 1856. The registration figures include many enterprises, perhaps 20 to 25%, which were stillborn, having failed to commence operation or raise their capital. Perhaps another equally large segment began operations but expired within one year. Few CPAs survived more than a decade. As in the case of partnerships, there was a built-in bias against CPAs enjoying a long life, as both were tied, absolutely in the case of the partnership and closely in the case of the CPA to the life of the responsible partner or *gérant*. Certainly the drafters of the *Code* viewed the CPA more like a partnership, whose life span would be limited to a medium term (*e.g.*, five to ten years) and would end earlier with the death, incapacitation, or resignation of the *gérant*, rather than in terms of an SA whose life span was independent of the individuals who managed it. CPAs attempted to escape from this handicap by providing in the charter for the replacement of *gérants* who resigned or died, a practice that was widely adopted and secured acceptance in the courts. But if some enterprises were able to secure a life span independent of the life or pleasure of their *gérants*, most CPAs, whose managers possessed virtually absolute authority, were closely identified with an individual or individuals. Their name(s) became the legal name of the enterprise (*e.g.*, Schneider et Cie.) whereas SAs were denominated by the object of the enterprise (*e.g.*, Fonderies et Forges de l'Horme). Many CPAs also adopted names designating the object of the enterprise, though this did not constitute their **legal** name.

The great authority vested in the *gérant* was not without a positive appeal to some entrepreneurs. Unlike the board of directors of an SA (*conseil d'administration*), which could determine policy and hire and fire the managers, the surveillance council (*conseil de surveillance*) of a CPA had only the right to verify the accounts presented by the *gérant* to the stockholders.[8] Certainly the Schneiders of the giant metallurgical concern at Le Creusot preferred, and maintained, the CPA over the SA. This was the case with other enterprises, including the smaller Allevard firm, which specialized in the manufacture of railroad equipment, where under a succession of three *gérants* from 1842 to 1905 the CPA was maintained because it suited the *gérants* not to have to answer to a board of directors. Only in 1905 with the death of Charles Pinat did the surveillance council decide to pass over the candidacy of his son Noel and transform the enterprise into an SA.[9] The

8   Surveillance councils became a normal institution in most CPAs even before the law of 1856 made them mandatory.
9   Pierre Léon, "Crises et adaptations de la métallurgie alpine, l'usine d'Allevard (1864-1914)," *Cahiers d'histoire*, VIII (1963), pp. 25 and 143-44.

CPA lent itself to family control of an enterprise. Another motive for the change of Allevard from a CPA to an SA was the desire to increase equity capital. If some entrepreneurs might prefer the CPA, stockholders generally did not. Stockholders in CPAs with poor dividend records usually blamed management and regretted their impotence to effect changes in policy and personnel.

The freeing of the SA form in 1867, completing what the restrictive law of 1856 had begun, reduced the CPA to a minor role. Among existing CPAs, a vacancy in the post of *gérant* afforded the stockholders an opportunity to transform the enterprise. And some *gérants* willingly traded their omnipotence and unlimited liability for authority derived from a board of directors and limited liability. CPAs before 1867 ranged in size from small to some quite large enterprises, unlike the SAs, which the Conseil d'Etat generally succeeded in limiting to large enterprises. The Paris and provincial Bourses quoted the shares of some of the larger CPAs.

In the four year period between mid-1863 and mid-1867, 338 SARLs were created; they were, in effect, SAs limited to a maximum capital of 20 MF, but free of the necessity of government authorization. SARLs varied widely in size from the Crédit Lyonnais, capitalized at the maximum of 20 MF, and the large locomotive manufacturing firm of Fives-Lille, capitalized at 6 MF, both of which were listed on the Paris Bourse, to quite small enterprise since the law of 1863 fixed no minimum size. Because of their recent vintage, a majority of them were probably still around in 1867. A reasonable guess would be that in 1867 France possessed approximately 1,250 joint-stock companies, comprising about 200 SAs, 800 CPAs and 250 SARLs.

Traditional forms of business organization declined only relatively with the rise of the joint-stock company. The proprietorship and partnership were not out-moded and continued to exist in ever larger numbers. At the beginning of the 19th century the joint-stock enterprise was a rare phenomenon generally regarded with fear and distrust; by 1867 it had become acclimated and had established its legitimacy in the eyes of most people. And by 1867, the joint-stock company already overshadowed the traditional forms of business organization in importance, both in the total volume of their capital and by the strategic position they occupied in the nation's economy. The joint-stock company dominated all sectors of the economy in which large size was necessary or advantageous, and it had acquired a strategic foothold in many other sectors where big was not necessarily better. The dividing line where the joint-stock company's advantages turned to disadvantages was in dispute, with many contemporaries exaggerating the extent of the obstacles to the successful operation of corporate enterprise. They believed that individual entrepreneurs operating with their own money invariably possessed an advantage over hired managers using other people's money. Some compared the corporation to a democracy, with inherent problems of decision-making and committee rule, in contrast to the alleged expeditiousness of decision and action of monarchies. While contemporaries, following Adam Smith, tended to emphasize the extent of entrepreneurial and managerial problems in determining the realm of the corporation, a better key is the optimum size of a firm's capital. The corporation possessed a distinct advantage over traditional forms of enterprise where large amounts of capital were required, balanced advantages and disadvantages where capital requirements were moderate, and faced disadvantages when the capital requirements were small.

The impact of the corporation on the economy, society and government was not lost on contemporaries. Was it good or bad? Had corporations reached their zenith, or had they only entered the stage of youthful vigor? Would the concentration of capital create, or had it already created, a financial and industrial oligarchy that would displace, or had displaced, traditional political authority? Opinions were many and varied. The operation of the law of 1867 would provide some answers to these questions, and it would raise many others.

The Fruits of Free Incorporation, 1867-1897

The law of 1867 provided the opportunity to utilize the corporate form of business organization without undergoing the lengthy and uncertain process involved in government authorization. The initial result was an immediate rise in the creation of SAs (see Table 1.1) from an annual average of 14 for the period 1842-1866 to an average of 219 per year for the period 1868-1878. Part of this rise was probably due to a decline in the creation of CPAs,[10] which averaged 128 per year between 1857-1867, as enterprises that formerly employed the CPA form were now free to become SAs. Also some existing CPAs and SARLs took advantage of the new law to transform themselves into SAs, and some previously authorized SAs transformed themselves into "free" SAs, which was forced upon them when their charters expired, but many SAs did so earlier for the convenience of amending their charters easily, or to escape unwanted restrictions in their charters. A flight from the CPA and the transformation of existing CPAs, SARLs and SAs into "free" SAs, accounted for many early incorporations under the new law, but, notwithstanding these transformations, incorporations reached

---

[10] Official statistics for the period 1868-1877 do not distinguish between the corporate type of *commandite* (CPA) and the partnership type of *commandite* (*société en commandite simple*).

a higher plateau, in spite of the countervailing impact of the Franco-Prussian War and the depression of the mid-1870s.

A boom in incorporations followed (see Graph 1.1). For the five year period 1879-1883, formation of SAs more than tripled over the previous eleven years (703 per year as compared with 219 per year) reaching levels that were not to be attained or surpassed until the end of the century. The single year 1881 saw the formation of 976 SAs, a figure not to be surpassed until 1899. Even after the collapse of the boom, the new level of company formation was on a higher plateau than for the period preceding the boom. From 1884 through 1890, formation of SAs fluctuated from a low of 295 (1887) to a high of 374 (1890). The upward trend continued during the years 1891-1897 with foundings ranging from a low of 401 (1893) to a high of 561 (1897).

Graph 1.1   Formation of *Sociétés Anonymes*, 1868-1897

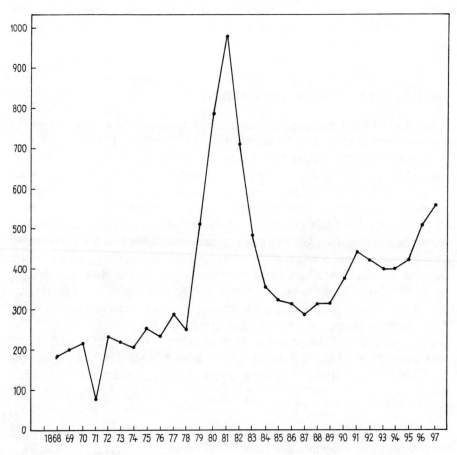

Fluctuations in the formation of SAs are a reasonably accurate mirror of general economic fluctuations, with an exaggeration in the amplitude of the ups and downs when compared with François Crouzet's index of industrial production,[11] and with a year or so lag when compared with the fluctuations of the Bourse, both on the upside and the downside. This was apparent during the boom of the late 1870s, which culminated in 1882. The boom in the economy was already underway for at least a year before it was reflected in company formations; similarly, the decline in incorporations lagged during the ensuing depression. This lag is to be accounted for by the time it takes to plan and to promote an SA. The result is that many new companies appear on the scene after their prospects for success have dimmed.

The increase in incorporations took place during a period when slow growth was the order of the day for the French economy following the high growth rates of the 1850s and 1860s that preceded it, and the resumption of high growth rates at the end of the 19th century. Behind this slowdown lay the end of massive investment for the construction of domestic railroads, which adversely affected a host of industries supplying railroad material. Replacement of losses suffered during the Franco-Prussian War and government expenditures under the Freycinet Plan helped to cushion the blow and delay the effects until the early 1880s. According to François Caron, the high level of investment during the 1870s was maintained primarily through the large retained earnings from the 1850s and 1860s.[12] But the end of extensive railroad construction was not the sole cause. A slump in agriculture, exacerbated by the phylloxera epidemic, occurred. There was also a decline in the growth of French exports, attributable to the rise of protectionism, and in the view of some, to the unwillingness of French businessmen to pursue an aggressive export policy. The ease with which SAs could be founded sustained the boom of the late 1870s and early 1880s, just as the earlier booms of the 1830s and 1850s were based upon the CPA. A distinguishing feature of this boom from the two earlier ones was the central role played by the Parisian and regional stock exchanges.

[11] François Crouzet, "Essai de construction d'un indice annuel de la production industrielle française au XIXe siècle," *Annales: Economies, Sociétés, Civilisations*, XXV (1970), p. 96.

[12] In *The Cambridge Economic History of Europe*, Vol. VIII, Part 1, Peter Mathias and M. M. Postan, eds., *The Industrial Economies: Capital, Labour, and Enterprise* (Cambridge, 1978), p. 273.

Table 1.1 Formation of *Sociétés Anonymes* and *Sociétés en Commandites par Actions*, 1868-1897

Year	SAs	CPAs	Year	SAs	CPAs
1868	191		1883	482	117
1869	200		1884	363	90
1870	223		1885	325	89
1871	83		1886	319	91
1872	239		1887	295	84
1873	220		1888	324	62
1874	214		1889	324	80
1875	253		1890	374	70
1876	239		1891	446	84
1877	290	71	1892	425	63
1878	256	80	1893	401	61
1879	511	120	1894	403	60
1880	797	129	1895	423	66
1881	976	143	1896	510	60
1882	738	156	1897	561	79

Sources: *Annuaire statistique de la France, Annuaire d'économie politique et de la statistique,* and *Compte général de l'administration de la justice civile et commerciale,* annual volumes.

Although figures for the period 1868-1876 are lacking, it is almost certain that the CPA continued the decline that had already begun when the restrictive law of 1856, and the depression of the late 1850s, dramatically decreased the use of this form of business organization. Although the law of 1867 removed a few of the onerous restrictions, it placed the CPA on an equal footing with the SA concerning the minimum value of shares, the total subscription of capital, and the minimum of one-quarter to be paid in. The basic difference between the two forms was reduced to one of governance, since both were subjected to the same requirements and formalities. As a result, the CPAs continued their slow downward trend, except for a brief spurt (1879-1883), through the period 1868-1897. If taken in relation to the total number of corporations founded, the decline of the CPAs was more pronounced; during the 1890s (1890-1897) the CPA accounted for only 13.3% of all corporations as compared with 21.9% for the period 1877-1889. CPAs retained greater popularity in the provinces than in the Paris area.

This decline puzzled some contemporaries, particularly those who continued to believe that the CPA afforded superior leadership. The admonitions of Adam Smith on corporate management and convictions about the superiority of the *l' oeil du maître* died hard. The question of whether or not the CPA was better suited than the SA for industrial enterprises was debated at a meeting of the liberal Société d'Economie Politique of Paris in 1886.[13] Léopold Hervieux argued pragmatically that the answer was obviously no, given the smaller number of CPAs as compared with SAs. Several speakers (Adolphe Coste, Alfred Neymarck, and Charles Lyon-Caen) emphasized the superiority of the SA for large enterprises, though they believed the CPA was useful for small or medium-size enterprises. On the other side, Alphonse Courtois and Emile Cheysson stressed the superiority of leadership in the CPA. Cheysson characterized the leadership in an SA as unstable and irresponsible. He also argued that the CPA was suited to large enterprise, citing the example of Le Creusot. Whatever the reason, the CPA no longer played more than a marginal role.

Beginning in 1889, figures for the capitalization of new corporations are available. (Table 1.2) These figures also include the capitalization of cooperatives (*sociétés à capital variable*). Since the maximum capital of a co-op at the time of its founding was limited to 200,000 francs (and few approached this magisterial figure), their impact on the total capitalization for joint-stock companies is relatively small. Incorporations did not necessarily involve raising new capital, or issuing shares for public sale, since many family firms incorporated simply to secure the benefits of limited liability. The average size of new corporations (SAs and CPAs) was small (about 900,000 francs), which reflects the presence of a large number of small family firms.

Table 1.2 Nominal Capital of New Joint-Stock Companies: SAs, CPAs, and Co-ops, 1889-1897

Year	Number	SAs	CPAs	Co-ops	Total Nominal Capital (million francs)
1889	449	324	80	45	449.8 (for 365 companies only)
1890	487	374	70	43	427.5
1891	620	446	84	90	533.9
1892	536	425	63	48	608.2
1893	532	401	61	70	323.9
1894	594	403	60	131	459.4

13 *L'Economiste français*, 9 Oct. 1886, pp. 436-38.

Year	Number	SAs	CPAs	Co-ops	Total Nominal Capital (million francs)
1895	635	423	66	146	499.6
1896	710	510	60	140	394.9
1897	805	561	79	165	540.2

Sources: *Annuaire statistique de la France* and *Annuaire d'économie politique et de la statistique*, annual volumes.

The Seine Department (Paris) led other departments in incorporations by a large margin accounting for annually between one-third to more than one-half of incorporations. (Table 1.3) Not only was Paris a large commercial and industrial center, but it was the leading financial center, and it was for this reason that regional enterprises established their seat in Paris. Enterprises incorporated in the provinces normally drew upon local sources for their capital.

Table 1.3 Formation of SAs: Paris (Seine) and Rest of France, at Three Year Intervals, 1879-1897

Year	Paris (Seine)	Rest of France	Total	Paris % (Seine)
1879	260	251	511	51%
1882	314	424	738	43%
1885	115	210	325	35%
1888	109	186	295	37%
1891	199	247	446	45%
1894	200	203	403	50%
1897	263	301	561	47%

Sources: *Annuaire d'économie politique et de la statistique* and *Compte général de l'administration de la justice civile et commerciale*, annual volumes.

Following the Seine Department, four other departments, all with major commercial or industrial centers, led in incorporations: Rhône (Lyon), Seine-Maritime (Rouen-Le Havre), Nord (Lille and other industrial towns), and Bouches de Rhône (Marseille) — see Table 1.4. Lyon, Lille, and Marseille also possessed their own Bourses that listed shares of local companies.

Table 1.4 Creation of SAs for Selected Departments, 1878-1885

Year	France	Seine	Rhône	Seine-Mar.	Nord	B. de R.
1878	256	119	15	15	16	9
1879	511	260	31	13	13	12
1880	797	482	21	23	10	21
1881	976	489	25	29	42	31
1882	738	314	25	33	18	29
1883	482	213	30	· 19	18	11
1884	363	127	14	17	15	9
1885	325	115	11	17	7	13

Source: *Compte général de l'administration de la justice civile et commerciale,* annual volumes.

A *Belle Epoque* for the Corporation, 1898-1913

The period 1898-1913, by contrast to the period 1868-1897, was one of accelerated economic growth, and the formation of corporations reflects this growth (Table 1.5). The average number of incorporations jumped from 380 per year for the 30 year period 1868-1897 to 953 per year for the period 1898-1913, achieving a new plateau. There were two booms, a short one, 1898-1901 and a longer one beginning in 1907 and continuing until the outbreak of the war (Graph 1.2). Starting in 1907, incorporations attained a sustained annual level of over 1,000. The founding of CPAs decreased slightly, from 88 per year for the period 1877-1897 to 82 per year for the period 1898-1913, but CPAs declined still further as a percentage of all SAs. This decline was sharpest in the Paris area, with CPAs retaining a certain favor in the provinces. The dominance of the Paris area for incorporations, already noted above for the preceeding period, continued. 48% of all SAs were founded in the Seine Department for the period 1898-1913.

Table 1.5 Formation of *Sociétés Anonymes* and *Sociétés en Commandites par Actions,* 1898-1913

Year	SAs	CPAs		Year	SAs	CPAs
1898	841	85		1903	601	88
1899	1,042	88		1904	638	64
1900	895	85		1905	836	67
1901	723	83		1906	823	69
1902	663	71		1907	1,113	90

Year	SAs	CPAs	Year	SAs	CPAs
1908	1,002	100	1911	1,226	91
1909	1,092	68	1912	1,328	114
1910	1,174	90	1913	1,255	66

Sources: *Annuaire statistique de la France* and *Annuaire d'économie politique et de la statistique*, annual volumes.

Graph 1.2 Formation of *Sociétés Anonymes*, 1898-1913

Incorporation of SAs from 1891 through 1895 ranged from a high of 446 (1891) to a low of 401 (1893). In 1896, the number of new SAs increased to 510, and in 1897 reached 561, though the annual average capitalization of SAs for 1891-1895 and 1896-1897 remained about the same. The year 1898 witnessed the inauguration of a new boom with the founding of 841 SAs, but the nominal capitalization of all incorporations (including 85 CPAs and 159 co-ops) jumped from 540 MF in 1897 to 1,429 MF in 1898 (See Table 1.6). In 1899, SAs pushed over the 1,000 level for the first time, and the total capitalization of all joint-stock companies leaped to a record of almost 2.7 billion francs. There were declines in 1900 and 1901, but levels of incorporations and capitalization remained much higher than during 1891-1897. Actually the boom was over by 1900, but incorporations displayed their usual stickiness, as noted before, on the downward side. From 1902 to 1906, incorporations stagnated, but at a level higher than for 1891-1897, both for the number of SAs and the total nominal capital. 1907 inaugurated an almost continuous boom until the outbreak of the war, with the creation of SAs regaining and maintaining the 1,000 level and with total nominal capital averaging over 1 billion francs annually for the whole period (though 1908 and 1909 showed substantial drops in nominal capitalization of new firms).

Table 1.6 Nominal Capital of New Joint-Stock Companies: SAs, CPAs, and Co-ops, 1898-1913

Year	Number	SAs	CPAs	Co-ops	Total Nominal Capital (MF)
1898	1,085	841	85	159	1,429.0
1899	1,291	1,042	88	161	2,674.4
1900	1,138	895	85	158	992.8
1901	964	723	83	158	1,266.6
1902	919	663	71	185	560.5
1903	855	601	88	166	351.5
1904	892	638	64	190	458.5
1905	1,112	836	67	209	649.9
1906	1,111	823	69	219	629.6
1907	1,391	1,113	90	188	1,084.0
1908	1,364	1,002	100	262	636.5
1909	1,319	1,092	68	159	644.6
1910	1,678	1,174	90	414	975.3

Year	Number	SAs	CPAs	Co-ops	Total Nominal Capital (MF)
1911	1,734	1,226	91	417	1,246.6
1912	1,758	1,328	114	316	1,085.3
1913	1,566	1,255	66	245	1,401.9

Sources: *Annuaire statistique de la France* and *Annuaire d'économie politique et de la statistique*, annual volumes.

Contributing to the boom in incorporations for the period 1898-1913 were general economic conditions both domestic and worldwide. Additions to the world's stock of gold reversed the deflationary trend evident since 1873. France also participated in the growth of international trade, contributed by the increasing sums devoted to armament by the major, and minor, powers. The appearance and growth of new industries (electricity and automobiles) provided a number of dynamic sectors of rapid growth. The generation and distribution of electricity, electric tramways, electrical equipment industries, and electro-metallurgy provided opportunities for huge new investment, as did the automobile industry in which France took a leading role.

Official statistics for 1898 provide valuable information concerning the total number of corporations in existence, their sectoral distribution, their nominal capitalization, the market value of their stocks, and the value of their bonds at maturity[14] (Tables 1.7 and 1.8). In 1898 there existed 6,325 joint-stock companies. Unfortunately, the types of joint-stock companies are not differentiated and include co-ops as well as SAs and CPAs. If we estimate the number of co-ops at 525,[15] the remaining 5,800 companies were divided between SAs and CPAs. Based upon the number of foundings of these two types of companies, and assuming the life expectancy of SAs was higher than CPAs, it may be estimated that there were approximately 5,100 SAs and 700 CPAs in 1898. When compared with the estimate above of the number of joint-stock enterprises in existence in 1867 (1,250, comprising 800 CPAs, 200 SAs and 250 SARLs), the number more than quadrupled in 30 years. The number of SAs increased enormously, CPAs declined slightly, and the SARLs probably disappeared.[16]

---

[14] The survey includes figures on borrowing (other than by issuing bonds) by corporations, but they are far too low to inspire any confidence. Also, it would be interesting to know how the market value of non-listed securities was calculated.

[15] For the period 1889-1898, the founding of co-ops averaged 103 per year, with foundings more than doubling beginning in 1894. Co-ops were particularly prone to a short life.

[16] A few may have survived until 1898, but most, like the Compagnie de Fives Lille and the Crédit Lyonnais, had transformed themselves into SAs.

Table 1.7 Negotiable Securities Issued by Corporations, 1898
(billion francs)

	Total Nominal Value	Market Value Listed Stocks	Market Value Non-listed Stocks	Total
Stocks	13.5	9.1	5.3	14.4
	Value at Maturity			Market Value
Bonds	29.6			27.4
Total	43.1			41.8

Source: *Annuaire statistique de la France*, XXI (1900), pp. 222-23.

The total nominal capitalization of all joint-stock companies was approximately 13.5 billion francs,[17] probably four to six times greater than in 1867. The market value of the shares amounted to 14.4 billion francs, of which 9.1 billion were the shares of public corporations that were listed on the Paris and regional Bourses. (See Table 1.7.) Some 5.3 billion francs were in shares of non-listed corporations, most of which were family enterprises, or closely held corporations. These figures testify to the strength of "family capitalism" in France. In banking, commerce, manufacturing and food processing, the capital of non-listed corporations was greater than those of listed companies (Table 1.8). Of course, many of the listed corporations were controlled by a family or a small group, in spite of the tendency of ownership to become widely diffused.

Table 1.8 Corporations in 1898
(MF = million francs)

Sector	Number	Listed Shares Market Value	Nonlisted Shares Market Value	Bonds at Maturity
Mines	1,366	1,379MF	279MF	127MF
Food Processing	689	265	326	87
Chemicals	496	545	351	282
Metalworking	437	588	364	220
Manufacturing (other)	634	80	661	99
Utilities	176	273	90	180

[17] The exclusion of co-ops would have little effect on these figures since the capitalization of all existing co-ops probably did not exceed 5 MF.

Sector	Number	Listed Shares Market Value	Nonlisted Shares Market Value	Bonds at Maturity
Transport	454	4,135	402	17,342
Commerce	1,129	292	562	132
Banks and Insurance	1,169	1,245	2,145	6,012
Total	5,553	8,802MF	5,180MF	24,481MF

Source: *Annuaire statistique de la France*, XXI (1900), pp. 222-23. (Co-ops are included in these figures, but they were typically quite small companies.)

The transportation sector, dominated by railroads, remained the largest, accounting for one-third of the total share capital; banks were second with almost 3.4 billion francs. The only other sector topping the one billion level was mining (more than 1.6 billion francs). Chemicals, metallurgy, and commerce all fell between 750 MF to 1 billion francs, followed by other manufacturing (741 MF), food processing (591 MF), and utilities (363 MF). Railroads and banks accounted for most of the bonded indebtedness with the issue of bonds exceeding that of their equity capital by a wide margin. For other sectors the issue of bonds was an important but less substantial source of funds ranging from about 7% (mining) to 50% (utilities) of equity capital. Excluding the financial sector, there is a positive correlation between fixed capital requirements and bonded indebtedness, as well as a positive correlation between larger firms, listed firms, and bonded indebtedness. The capital of the 772 other firms not included in Table 1.8, encompassing such sectors as fishing and agriculture, totaled less than 400 MF.

When compared with the number and capitalization of corporations in the United Kingdom and Germany at this time, and in 1914, France occupied an intermediate position, lagging behind Britain and leading Germany (Table 1.9). The fact that of the three, Britain possessed the most liberal incorporation laws and Germany the most stringent, certainly had an effect, but it is certainly not the only reason.

Table 1.9 Corporations in the United Kingdom, France and Germany
c. 1898 and 1913

	Date	Number	Nominal Capital (billion francs)
UK	1898	25,267	34.5 (£1.38 billion)
	1913	60,754	60.7 (£2.43 billion)
France	1898	5,800	13.5
	1913	(13,340)	(20-25) estimated
Germany	1896	3,712	8.2 (6.8 billion marks)
	1909	5.222	17.6 (14.7 billion marks)

Sources: The figures for the UK and Germany are taken from the *Hand-worterbuch der Staatswissenschaften* 4th ed. (Jena 1923-28), I, pp. 149, 158 and 169. The French figures for 1913 are conservative estimates, based upon an estimated mortality rate of 30% for corporations existing in 1898, and of 40% for all corporations formed during the 15 year period 1899-1913. Currency conversions were at the rate of 1£ = 25 francs and 1 mark = 1.2 francs.

The statistics for this cross-country comparison are not without their pitfalls. The UK figures are for limited companies, while the French and German figures include both SAs and CPAs for France and the *Aktiengesellschaft* (AG) and *Kommanditgesellschaft auf Aktien* (KGaA) for Germany. They do not include the German *Gesellschaft mit Beschranken Haftung* (GMBH), which was introduced in 1892, enabling family firms and partnerships to secure the benefits of limited liability. Some large enterprises employed this form, which did not exist in France until it was introduced, via Alsace-Lorraine, in 1925. The UK figures do not include railroads and tramways, and to the extent that they were not private enterprises, they are largely absent from the German figures also. On the other hand, France had a much smaller population than both the UK and Germany. But in spite of imperfections in the comparison, it is sufficiently accurate to indicate that France continued to lead Germany in the utilization of the corporation. This is borne out by examining incorporations for the period 1901-1910 (Table 1.10).

Table 1.10   Incorporations for United Kingdom, France and Germany:
Annual Average, 1901-1910

	Number	Total Nominal Cap. (French francs)	Avg. Cap. per Company (French francs)
UK	4,748	3.433 million	728,000
France (SAs)	866	700 million	820,000
Germany (AGs)	157	299 million	1,905,000

Sources: *Handworterbuch der Staatswissenschaften* 4th ed. (Jena 1923-28), I, pp. 155-56 and 169. The UK figures include a few unlimited companies and limited companies without a declared nominal capital. The average capitalization of French SAs was determined by subtracting 3% from the total capitalization in Table 1.6 to allow for the capitalization of CPAs and co-operatives.

Germany lagged behind both France and the UK in numbers and total capitalization, though the average size of the German corporation was larger. Consistent with the degree of restrictiveness of company law, the mortality rate for corporations was lowest in Germany and highest in the UK.

Unlike England, the lack of a central registry for all corporations in France leaves the historian at a disadvantage in establishing the identity of new incorporations. However, the finance law of 30 January 1907, requiring that all new companies issuing shares for public sale publish certain information in an annex to the *Journal Officiel*, offers some assistance. Although it generally failed to serve its intended purpose of providing vital information to investors, and it was regarded by the companies as an expensive nuisance, it does provide a partial record for the historian. An examination of the volume for 1913 shows that 741 corporations issuing shares to the public were founded.[18] Of a total of 1,321 corporations founded in 1913, only 56% issued shares for public sale. The rest were, in effect, "private" corporations (Table 1.11). Among "private" corporations, most (87%) were small (capitalized under 1 MF) family enterprises. According to an informed contemporary, Jacques Hatt, France, unlike Germany, had no need for the *Gesellschaft mit Beschranken Haftung*, which was created to provide limited liability for family enterprises, because family enterprise could utilize the SA form.[19] The "private" SA satisfied both the penchant for secrecy and the

[18] This includes some companies founded toward the end of 1912, which appeared in the 1913 volume, but omits some companies founded at the end of 1913, which appeared in the 1914 volume. It is assumed that any actual discrepancy for 1913 would be small.

[19] Jacques Hatt, "Faut-il adopter la société à responsabilité limitée allemande?" Louis Mathieu, ed., *Documents du Congrès Juridique International des Sociétés par Action et des Sociétés Coopératives, Bruxelles 1910* (2 vols., Louvain, 1910), I, pp. 179-80. Hatt was also the

desire for continuing family control. Because no shares were issued for public sale, the private SA was not required to make public its financial statements. SAs that issued shares to the public had no control over who purchased them, but the private SA, in its charter, could restrict the transfer of shares to insure continuing family control. One way was to subject the transfer of shares to the approval of the board of directors. The charter of the Peugeot company limited the transmission of shares to male family members.[20]

However, the GMBH did possess certain advantages for small family enterprise over the SA. It could be formed with as few as two persons, instead of the seven required for an SA. This was not an insuperable obstacle as token shares could be given to wives, children, or trusted employees. A more serious obstacle were the substantial costs in forming an SA, which effectively discouraged enterprises capitalized at less than several hundred thousand francs. In contrast, the average capitalization of GMBHs founded in Germany in 1909 was 110,000 marks.[21] Few firms of this size in France became SAs.

Table 1.11 Public and "Private" Corporations Founded in 1913[22]

	Public	"Private"	Total
SAs	705	550	1,255
CPAs	36	30	66
Total	741	580	1,321

Sources: *Annuaire statistique de la France*, 1913 and *Journal Officiel, Bulletin des annonces légales et obligatoire à la charge des sociétés financières*, 1913.

Among medium-size and large companies (capitalized at 1 MF or more), 187 of 262 (71%) were public corporations (Table 1.12).

---

author of *La Société en responsabilité limitée en droit allemand contemporain* (Paris, 1908). The 3rd International Congress on Corporations, held in connection with the Brussels World's Fair of 1910, devoted a session to the GMBH and its usefulness for other countries.

[20] Daniel Henri, "Capitalisme familial et gestion industrielle au XIXe siècle," *Revue française de gestion*, No. 70 (1988), pp. 148-49.

[21] Albert Leroi, "Des Sociétés anonymes privées," Louis Mathieu, ed., *Documents du Congrès Juridique International des Sociétés par Actions*, I, p. 169.

[22] The figures for "private" SAs were calculated by subtracting the figures for public SAs in the 1913 *Bulletin* from the total for all SAs in the *ASF* for 1913.

Table 1.12 Public and "Private" Corporations According to Size, 1913

Capital	Public	Private	Total
Under 1 MF	554	505	1.059
1-5 MF	172	65	237
Over 5-10 MF	11	2	13
Over 10 MF	4	8	12
TOTAL	741	580	1,321

Sources: *Annuaire statistique de la France*, 1913 and *Journal Officiel, Bulletin des annonces légales et obligatoire à la charge des sociétés financières*, 1913.

Of these 180 were SAs and 7 were CPAs. All of the large corporations (capitalized at more than 5 MF) were SAs. Among corporations capitalized at more than 5 MF to (and including) 10 MF, 11 of 13 were public companies. But only 4 of the 12 companies capitalized for more than 10 MF were public companies. The total capitalization of these 4 companies was 205 MF, while the capitalization of the 8 large "private" corporations was 419 MF. This is somewhat misleading because most large "private" corporations were founded by promoters, banks, or groups, who fulfilled all the formalities of foundation and who subscribed all the shares themselves, with a view of a later sale to the public at a premium.

Many of the medium-size (1 to 5 MF) and almost all of the small (under 1 MF) "private" companies were either family or closely held firms which were adopting the corporate form of business organization to take advantage of limited liability, or to solve managerial problems. In the later case, which is often underestimated, the corporate form enabled individuals to retire from active management of an enterprise. The large number of family, or closely held, firms adopting the corporate form of business organization was not peculiar to France. The practice existed in other European countries and was widespread in both Britain and Germany.[23] The spectacular rise of the giant corporation has tended to obscure the persistence and importance of family firms.

Most of the medium-size and large public corporations (167 of 187) called for total payment on their shares. Of the remainder, 19 called the minimum of one-quarter, and one called one-half. This indicates not only a

---

[23] Jürgen Brockstedt, "Family Enterprise and the Rise of Large-Scale Enterprise in Germany (1871-1914)" in Akio Okochi and Shigeaki Yasouka, eds., *Family Enterprise in the Era of Industrial Growth* (Tokyo, 1984), pp. 237-67; Peter L. Payne, "Family Enterprise in Britain: An Historical and Analytical Survey," in Ibid., pp. 171-97; Daniel Henri, "Capitalisme familial et gestion industrielle au XIXe Siècle," *Revue française de gestion*, No. 70 (1988), pp. 141-50.

reluctance on the part of the public to buy shares with unpaid calls, but also a desire of the companies to issue the popular bearer shares, which by law had to be fully paid up. Some shares were issued at a premium. The 1,000 francs par value shares of the Banque Renauld of Nancy, a former CPA which was transforming itself into an SA and increasing its capital from 20 to 40 MF, were issued at 1,200 francs. The 500 francs shares of the Banque Nationale de Crédit, founded by the Comptoir d'Escompte de Mulhouse and the Banque Française pour le Commerce et l'Industrie and capitalized at 100 MF, were issued at 625 francs. Incorporations in 1913 also reflected a great interest in foreign and colonial ventures: Among the 187 medium and large companies, at least 41 were founded for direct investment or trade either with the colonies (18 companies), or foreign countries (23 companies). Among these companies were 7 banks, 5 trading companies, 9 mining or oil drilling ventures and 6 real estate companies.

By 1914, corporations had come to dominate the economy; the history of the corporation passed, beginning with the enactment of the law of 1867, into a new stage characterized by the freedom to found SAs without governmental authorization. The result was a huge increase in incorporations, and the spread of the SA to sectors which government officials hitherto had denied access. The SA became the chief vehicle for the developing capitalist economic system, its role being such that it is not an exaggeration to view the period as the triumph of corporate capitalism. But the operation of the law of 1867 was not without its pitfalls. Speculative excesses, frauds and the comparison of the French corporate law with that of other countries called into question the basic principles as well as individual provisions of the law of 1867. The next chapter deals with the ensuing debate.

CHAPTER II

THE DEBATE OVER CORPORATE LAW

Il ne manque pas de légistes auxquels toute société semble suspect.

Paul Leroy-Beaulieu, 1886

The law of 1867, which formed the basis for French company law for the next hundred years, did not terminate the debate over the conditions for founding and operating corporations. The belief persisted in some quarters that the law was too restrictive; others thought it was too liberal whilst some even advocated returning to government authorization for SAs. The first attempt at reform occurred in 1875 in the wake of a financial crisis. A few years later, the collapse of the boom of 1879-1882 gave the restrictionists the upper hand for almost a decade, and they attempted to push through a comprehensive overhaul of the law. But the liberal view dominated from the 1890s until the Rochette scandal after 1907 put them on the defensive. In spite of the ebb and flow of public opinion, neither group was able to overcome legislative inertia to effect major changes in the law of 1867. However, the debates during these four decades are an integral part of the history of the corporation, reflecting the hopes and fears about the youthful corporate Goliath that was transforming the structure of the French economy.

First Attempt at Reform

The initial challenge to the law of 1867 resulted from large scale defaults on bonds of regional railroad lines. Many local and regional lines failed to generate sufficient revenues to meet interest payments, which is why the major lines had declined to build them in the first place. Another reason for the defaults was that the troubled companies were highly leveraged, issuing bonds several times the amount of their equity capital. The bonded debt of

26

some companies exceeded their equity capital by a margin of about three to one, which struck government officials as excessive. By 1875, for example, the Charentes line had realized just under 20 MF by its shares but over 59 MF through the issue of bonds, and the Vendee line 8.4 MF from its shares and over 30 MF from bonds. The eight regional lines in France that formed part of the already troubled railroad and financial empire of the Belgian promoter, Simon Philippart, had, by the end of 1874, issued 258.7 MF worth of bonds and only 138.5 MF of stock.[1] There was nothing new about this method of financing railroads as most of the major lines constructed during the Second Empire issued bonds in amounts far exceeding their equity capital. What was new was the ruin of railroad bondholders on an unprecedented scale.

In April 1875, Minister of Justice Jules Dufaure appointed an extraparliamentary commission, composed mostly of high ranking civil servants, and presided over by Ernest Picard, to reform the law of 1867.[2] Dufaure advised the commission to deal with only essential reforms and to keep the bill short in order not to require too much of the National Assembly's time. The minister of public works proposed that the bill should prohibit the issuing of bonds in amounts larger than the paid-in capital of a company,[3] a proposal that the commission incorporated in its bill. The commission discussed the possibility of requiring government authorization for all companies that were either subsidized or receiving interest guarantees from the state or departments. This proposal was rejected because, as a member of the commission, A. Vavasseur argued, the units of government according the subsidies already possessed sufficient powers to force compliance with whatever restrictions they saw fit to require.[4] One member of the commission, Croizette Desnoyers, feared that restricting the issue of domestic bonds might drive French savings into foreign bonds where the same safeguards did not apply, but the majority were not worried by a flight of capital. As a high ranking official in the Ministry of Finance, Dutilleul, expressed it: "let our money go where it wishes."

---

[1] G. Kurgan-van Hentenryk, *Rail, finance et politique: Les entreprises Philippart, 1865-1890* (Brussels, 1982), p. 219.

[2] In addition to Picard, a prominent republican legislator, and A. Vavasseur, a lawyer who served as secretary, there were: A. de Courcy, a director of the Compagnie d'Assurances Générales; Croizette Desnoyers, Inspecteur-Général des Ponts et Chaussées; Dumoustier de Frédilly, Directeur du Commerce Intérieur at the Ministry of Commerce; Dutilleul, Directeur-Général du Mouvement des Fonds at the Ministry of Finance; Langlois de Neuville, Chef de Division at the Ministry of Public Works; Levavasseur, Directeur-Général de l'Enregistrement des Domaines et du Timbre; Manuel, substitut au Procureur Général près la Cour d'appel of Paris.

[3] F[12]6833A Min. of Public Works to Min. of Commerce, 20 April 1875.

[4] F[12]6833A P. V. of the Commission. The Commission held 7 meetings between 10 April and 7 May 1875.

On other matters, Vavasseur proposed that in the interest of better disclosure a special publication be created in which all corporations would be required to publish certain basic information, a proposal the commission adopted unanimously. The bill proposed by the commission would also increase from 2 to 5 years the period of liability of original subscribers for calls; no bearer shares were to be issued until all the shares were completely paid-up (instead of one-half). The commission agreed to provisions making it easier to amend charters, but a plea by Vavasseur to extend the rights of bondholders, by recognizing assemblies of bondholders and giving them the power to reject the issue of additional bonds, was rejected. The commission could not agree on a proposal to insure that stockholders' meetings were composed of "real" stockholders (fears about rigged stockholders' meetings received much attention) though a range of solutions were discussed.[5] The National Assembly went out of existence before the bill was taken up, but Vavasseur, who served as secretary of the commission, published his own, longer, reform proposal the following year as a guide to future legislation.[6] The law of 11 June 1880 strictly regulated the issue of bonds by regional railroads and tramways, but the other proposals remained, in one form or another, on the agenda for many years.

Bontoux's Legacy

The spectacular crash of an investment bank, the Union Générale, in 1882 symbolized the end of a classic speculative boom that began in 1879.[7] The founding of SAs on a hitherto unprecedented scale gave this boom its particular character. From 1868 to 1878 the creation of SAs averaged 219 a year. In 1879, 511 SAs were founded, 797 in 1880, and 976 in 1881. The rise in the capitalization of new enterprises was even more spectacular. The nominal capital of new joint-stock companies and partnerships for the Paris area mirrored the rise and fall of the boom:[8]

1878	335 MF	1882	1,276 MF
1879	930 MF	1883	545 MF
1880	1,285 MF	1884	379 MF
1881	2,632 MF		

---

5   Ibid.

6   A. Vavasseur, *Un projet de loi sur les sociétés* (Paris, 1876).

7   The best account of the debacle is Jean Bouvier, *La Krach de l'Union Générale, 1878-1885* (Paris, 1960).

8   *Gazette des tribunaux*, 23 janv. 1881, pp. 82-83; 21 janv. 1883, p. 72; 22 janv. 1885, p. 72.

Approximately 80% of the totals were for SAs. For all of France the nominal capital of newly founded SAs in 1881 topped any year for the period 1868-1914.

The demand for capital during the boom was greatly swollen by existing corporations increasing their capitalization. The Union Générale increased its nominal capitalization (only one-quarter was called) from 25 to 50 MF in 1879, to 100 MF in 1881, and was in the process of adding another 50 MF in January 1882 when the end came. Another bank that exemplified the boom was the Crédit Général Français, founded in 1872 and capitalized at 1.2 MF, which between 1879 and 1882 increased its capital from 6 to 20, to 60, to 120 MF. One knowledgeable contemporary, Athanase Cucheval-Clarigny, estimated the combined total capital of newly founded companies and new issues of existing companies for 1880 at more than 4 billion francs.[9]

For 1881, Paul Leroy-Beaulieu, the editor of the *Economiste Français*, calculated that the 125 new issues of securities quoted on the Paris Bourse alone totaled more than 5 billion francs,[10] while Léon Say, who took over as Finance Minister in January 1882, cited an estimate of 7 billion francs for all new issues for 1881.[11]

In France the boom focused upon banks, insurance companies, real-estate companies, and gas and water companies, but much of the capital was for foreign investment as the activities of the Union Générale in the Austrian Empire and the Balkans amply illustrate. The number of new companies quoted on the Paris Bourse, including both domestic and foreign, doubled between 1877 and 1881, and issues of companies handled by the brokers of the unofficial *coulisse* increased even more.[12]

Although Paris and Lyon were the centers of the boom, the speculative mania spread throughout France, fueled by the publication of financial journals, most of which were products of the boom itself. It was the practice of the new investment banks to create or buy their own financial journal, though some financial journals reversed the process and transformed themselves into banks. It is estimated that there were 228 financial journals published in April 1881, in addition to the financial sections of 95 newspapers.[13] The annual subscription rate of most of these journals was low, often only 1 or 2 francs, a sum insufficient to cover the postage. The journals attracted a new clientele for buying shares, particularly in the provinces, and some installed hundreds of branch offices in small and medium-size towns,

---

9   A. Cucheval-Clarigny, "La Situation financière, le budget de 1882, la Banque de France et les sociétés financières," *Revue des deux mondes*, 1 Aug. 1881, p. 597.

10   J. Bouvier, *La Krach*, p. 29.

11   Ibid., pp. 130ff.

12   A. Bailleux de Marisy, "Moeurs financières de la France: les nouvelles sociétés foncières," *Revue des deux mondes*, 15 Nov. 1881, p. 434.

13   André Cochut, cited in J. Bouvier, *La Krach*, pp. 28-29.

acting as intermediaries in the buying of shares. In Nantes, at least 4 financial journals, all owned by banks, established branch offices offering brokerage services.[14]

The demand for capital being several times greater than French savings made a liquidation inevitable. The only question was where and when. In the pages of the *Journal des économistes*, in June 1881, Adolphe Blaise (des Vosges) predicted a disastrous crash.[15] He disliked the foreign ventures spawned by the boom, particularly singling out the activities of the Union Générale. The spark for the crash, he believed, could come from abroad. Cucheval-Clarigny, writing in the *Revue des deux mondes* in August 1881, foresaw a clearing of the market which could be either "slow and orderly," or "sudden and violent."[16] However, the boom still had a way to go before reaching its zenith. Share prices continued to rise. The shares of the Union Générale, on which only 125 francs had been called, were around 1,400 francs at mid-year; by the end of 1881, they stood at 2,815 francs. The collapse of inflated share prices on the Bourses of Paris and Lyon in January 1882, and the fall of the Union Générale in February summoned a return to reality. The crash left in its wake the usual disasters; Lyon, where the virus of speculation was particularly widespread, was hit hardest. The number of victims was greater and more dispersed than was the case with the earlier speculative booms of the late 1830s and the mid-1850s, which were mainly confined to Paris.

Within a few days after the failure of the Union Générale and the arrest for fraud of its chief, Eugène Bontoux, Minister of Justice Humbert appointed on 14 February 1882 an extraparliamentary commission to revise the law of 1867. Many deemed that the relatively unhindered creation of SAs under the law of 1867 was responsible for the excesses of the boom. Presided over by Senator J. Bozérian, the commission included the usual mixture of eminent men: parliamentarians (Bozérian and Charles Ferry, a deputy), law professors (Lyon-Caen of Paris and Louis Arnault, the reporter of the commission, from Toulouse), legists (Baudouin, later replaced by Monod, both members of the Cour de Cassation, Baudelot, a former president of the Commercial Tribunal of Paris, Louis Loew, a procureur at Paris and Vavasseur, the lawyer who played a major role on the reform commission of 1875), civil servants (Clamageran from the Conseil d'Etat, Girard from the Ministry of Commerce, Gonse from the Ministry of Justice, and Gay and Pallain from the Ministry of Finance), brokers (Moreau and

---

[14] A. Moron, *La Verité sur les journaux financières à bon marché* (Nantes, 1882), pp. 8-13.

[15] A. Blaise, "Un cote de l'histoire financière contemporaine, Le développement des établissements de crédit" *Journal des économistes*, 15 juin 1881, p. 333.

[16] A. Cucheval-Clarigny, "La Situation financière," *Revue des deux mondes*, 1 Aug. 1881, p. 603.

Lecomte — some revision of stock exchange law was also envisioned) and bankers (Alphonse Mallet, a regent of the Bank of France, Durieu, a director of the CIC, and Girod, a director of the Comptoir d'Escompte). The preponderance of civil servants and members of the legal profession insured a highly restrictive proposal.[17]

Even before the commission met, there existed a detailed catalogue of abuses and suggestions for legislative reform, which had appeared over the previous years. Two extreme viewpoints attracted some adherents. One of these would dispense with the provisions of the law of 1867 on SAs, and simply return to the pre-1867 system of government authorization.[18] The other presented by Emile Ollivier, who published a pamphlet early in 1882, later reprinted by the *Journal des économistes*,[19] advocated the same position he had taken at the time of the elaboration of the law of 1867. Ollivier proposed the repeal of both the provisions of the Code and the law of 1867. Businessmen should have complete freedom in shaping the forms of business enterprise, subject only to adequate disclosure. The repression of fraud should not be the subject of special legislation, always a favorite device of the restrictionists, but should be left to the common law.[20] A broad center group wanted to effect changes in the law of 1867, but this group covered a wide range of opinion from those who would simply make a few changes — though there was no agreement within this group over what those few changes should consist of — to those who would try to anticipate, and repress, every possible kind of fraud. The zeal of the latter represented a serious threat to legitimate business. Much of the criticism centered upon the manner in which companies were created, and the frauds perpetrated during the boom appeared to offer ample justification for their fears.

In 1867 the legislator tried to repress fraud by enacting into law the restrictions elaborated by the Conseil d'Etat during the years of government authorization, and by making it possible for stockholders to exercise the control formerly exercised by the Conseil d'Etat. But promoters learned how to elude the restrictions, while adhering to the letter, if not the spirit, of the law. The law provided for a stockholders' meeting prior to the definitive constitution of a company, where the stockholders would specifically debate and pass on the value of the fixed assets which the promoters would exchange for shares, and upon the compensation and other benefits that the

[17] Alfred Neymarck and others, including Roy, the president of the Chamber of Commerce of Paris criticized the lack of business representation on the commission. Alfred Neymarck, *Rapport sur les réformes de la loi de 1867 sur les sociétés* (Paris, 1882), p. 4.

[18] F. Malapert, "Les lois sur les sociétés par actions," *Journal des économistes*, 15 September 1880, pp. 340-55.

[19] "De la liberté des sociétés," *Journal des économistes*, 15 avril 1882, pp. 50-59, an abbreviated version of his *De la liberté des sociétés à propos de l'Union Générale* (Paris, 1882).

[20] Ibid., p. 59.

promoters would receive. All this was based upon the assumption that the interests of the stockholders would dictate careful consideration of these matters. The procedure was avoided by having the minimum of seven men form the company, often under the patronage of a financial institution. These seven men subscribed all the shares (paid in the mandatory one-quarter of the capital) and as shareholders approved the acquisition of fixed assets (often at an inflated value) in exchange for shares. They also passed upon the allocation of promotional costs to be paid to the founders, or other advantages, such as special shares for founders (*parts de fondateur*), which entitled them to a portion of the profits after the ordinary shareholders had received a certain amount. Thus the company could be legally constituted without a serious review by the ultimate stockholders. Only after the company had been legally constituted would the shares be sold to the public, and if the promoters did their job well, the shares would be sold at a premium, which also would go into the pockets of the promoters.

Temporary syndicates were often formed to centralize the sale of shares, insuring that they would be disposed of in an orderly fashion so as not to depress the market; the syndicate might also buy shares to stabilize the price. Profits from promotional activities could be high for banks and other promoters because the needed capital was tied up for only a limited time. For example, par value 500 francs shares with one-quarter called would require a capital outlay of 125 francs per share; if these shares were sold for 225 francs, a return of 100 francs per share, less promotional expenses including legal fees and subsidies to the press, could be realized.

The intention to defraud innocent shareholders was not the basis of all promotional activity, as many legists and civil servants imagined. These methods were employed by the most reputable banks (*e.g.*, Paribas, the Société Générale, and Rothschilds) which, even after their holdings in the new companies were reduced to token amounts, remained on the scene to help direct the future course of the enterprise (and to underwrite future stock and bond issues). Since the banks sold many or most of the shares of the companies they promoted to their own clients, the new enterprise had to have some substance as even the most reputable banks could not afford many mistakes. High premiums were not enjoyed by all, but were normally based upon the reputation of the sponsoring banks. Although the stereotypical picture of stockholders as a flock of dumb sheep will not bear careful scrutiny, during a boom promoters and investors alike tended to be carried along by the general euphoria. Normal caution was forgotten and new men and new money, animated by the "get rich quick" syndrome were drawn into an ever-rising market. In such a climate shady operators found many victims.

A survey of some of the main criticisms of company law affords an indication of abuses and remedies considered by the extraparliamentary commission, and subsequently by the Senate. In 1880, J. G. Courcelle-

Seneuil, a liberal economist, surveyed abuses in company promotion, particularly by banks.[21] For him, "the interest of the founding bank and that of the company are always different and often opposed."[22] Though, as a liberal, he was hesitant about the desirability of legislative intervention, he did suggest a number of reforms to alleviate abuses without unduly hindering business. He proposed that the capital value of all shares should be entirely called (instead of the one-quarter minimum); shares attributed in exchange for fixed assets should be non-negotiable for three years; no one should sit on more than one board of directors;[23] unions of bondholders should be permitted; and foreign companies should be subjected to the same requirements as French companies. No longer should French companies formed in Brussels, that "paradise of promoters" which required only 5% to be called on shares, be allowed to sell their shares in France. On the other hand, Courcelle-Seneuil proposed to free life-insurance companies from government authorization and, a radical proposal, to permit the free creation of banks of issue.

Just before the extraparliamentary commission was appointed, Alfred Neymarck, editor of *Le Rentier*, who no doubt hoped to be appointed to the commission, suggested changes in the law of 1867.[24] The assigning of an exaggerated value to fixed assets, over which the stockholders exercised no effective control, was one of the abuses to be corrected. Neymarck proposed that a neutral court-appointed assessor evaluate such assets. Neymarck also proposed to establish an effective system to verify payments for subscribed shares, to require more detailed and frequent (monthly) financial statements, to permit small shareholders to vote in stockholders' meetings, to quote only fully paid-up shares on the Bourse, and to prohibit bearer shares that were not fully paid-up. As was to be expected from the editor of *Le Rentier*, the emphasis was on the protection of shareholders, particularly small shareholders.

Similar suggestions came from the liberal financial journalist, Paul Leroy-Beaulieu, editor of the *Economiste Français*. Following the huge losses of railroad bondholders in the mid-1870s, Leroy-Beaulieu proposed from time to time ways to increase the power of surveillance of stock and bond holders

---

[21] "De la législation relative aux sociétés par actions," *Journal des économistes*, 15 August 1880, pp. 169-87.

[22] Ibid., p. 177.

[23] The cumulation of directorships resulted in the creation of an oligarchy, according to Courcelle-Seneuil. ". . . the control of almost all industry constituted as joint-stock companies in . . . France has been permitted to fall into the hands of about 400 persons, who levy on industry an enormous tribute, comparable to *droits féodaux*." Ibid., p. 183. No socialist writer put it more bluntly.

[24] A. Neymarck, *Les sociétés anonymes par actions, quelques réformes pratiques* (Paris, 1882).

over corporate enterprises. Bondholders should have the right to organize, and the right to examine the books of the enterprise.[25] The *censeurs*, charged with verifying company accounts for the stockholders, ought to be better paid, and drawn from the ranks of professional accountants. Financial statements should contain greater detail to prevent the carrying of fixed assets at inflated values. No one should be permitted to sit on more than one board of directors because of potential conflicts of interest. Where corporations have identical boards of directors, such as the Crédit Foncier and the Crédit Agricole, averred Leroy-Beaulieu, abuses are inevitable.[26] Senators and deputies should be prohibited from sitting on boards, unless they held the directorship prior to their election. Leroy-Beaulieu estimated that between 200 and 300 deputies and senators sat in corporate boardrooms, posts for which they were generally unfit, but which paid from 1,200 to 2,000 francs annually, and often much higher amounts in those companies where the directors received a percentage of the profits.[27]

As the boom of the late 1870s got underway, Leroy-Beaulieu, departing from his inveterate optimism, attacked the new speculative mania, evoking in the pages of the *Economiste Français* the hoary memory of John Law and the ill-famed rue Quincampoix; his prediction in 1879 of the crash was a little premature. Lucrative business opportunities, he wrote, were insufficient for the many new banks and insurance companies that were being created. The small size of many of the new enterprises was also criticized:

> . . . joint-stock companies are unsuited for modest enterprises; the SA is intended for large operations for which the individual proprietorship is inappropriate: a bank capitalized in the tens of millions, an enormous metallurgical enterprise, a huge transport line. Even the SA has its inconveniences because it is essentially wasteful; every SA suffers from a considerable waste of funds, but there are occasions where its services cannot be dispensed with or replaced.[28]

No doubt large organizations, corporations and state bureaucracies, are wasteful, but Leroy-Beaulieu's illusions about efficiency in the management of small enterprises is open to question.

---

[25] *Economiste français*, 24 August 1878, p. 227.

[26] Ibid., 13 Jan. 1878, pp. 33-34 and 9 Nov. 1878, pp. 610-11.

[27] Ibid., 21 July 1877, pp. 66-67 and 8 Nov. 1879, pp. 558-59. In 1882, Leroy-Beaulieu included the nobility along with politicians as candidates for directorships. Evidently the salary for these window dressing functions had increased to between 1,800 and 3,000 francs annually. At 18 to 25 members, Leroy-Beaulieu thought these boards were too large. He believed it would be better to have a knowledgeable board of 7 or 8 members receiving 8,000 to 15,000 francs. *Economiste français*, 18 Feb. 1882, p. 191. Alfred Neymarck noted in 1887 that military men, diplomats, deputies and senators were members of boards virtually *"de droit."* Out of 10 to 20 board members, usually only two or three had a grasp of the business, according to Neymarck. *Finances contemporaines*, VI (1911), pp. 67-71.

[28] *Economiste français*, 6 Sept. 1879, p. 297.

When the commission was beginning its work, the illustrious Société d'Economie Politique of Paris at its March 1882 meeting discussed the question of what changes "economic science" would propose for the law of 1867.[29] Apart from a general skepticism about the efficacy of governmental action, the responses showed that "economic science" did not speak with a single voice. While Alphonse Courtois, Jules Boucherot, and Comte Ciez-kowsky proposed that founders and directors of SAs be subjected to un-limited liability, Paul Leroy-Beaulieu rejected this proposal as one which would drive serious men from these posts, replacing them by straw men. Both Leroy-Beaulieu and Charles Limousin wanted legislation to guarantee the reality of the capital, liquid and fixed, of the company at the time of its foundation, but Boucherot argued that this was likely to be an illusory guarantee. Limousin proposed that owners of a single share be allowed to vote at stockholders' meetings, countered by Boucherot who believed that too much democracy at such meetings was bad. Other recommendations included fuller disclosure requirements and prohibition of bearer shares unless they were entirely paid-up.

Another discussion took place at the Chamber of Commerce of Paris, which submitted eight resolutions adopted by the Chamber to the Ministry of Commerce, on 23 May 1883.[30] The Chamber proposed that all shares should be in the name of the owner until completely paid-up, and that original subscribers remain liable for unpaid calls for two years after having sold their shares; no company should be allowed to issue new shares until the old shares were entirely paid-up. The subscription form for shares should be required to indicate the respective portion of cash and fixed assets in the company's capital; subscription forms for bonds should indicate the amount of unpaid calls on shares, and list any prior issues of bonds. Bond-holders should enjoy the same rights as stockholders to information con-cerning the company. The rights of commissioners, who represented stockholders, should be broadened to enable them to verify the company's activities. Finally, the Chamber approved fully paid up 100 francs shares for companies whose capital was 500,000 francs or less.

The extraparliamentary commission devoted its first six meetings to pre-paring a bill regulating the futures' market, but on 25 March it turned its attention to the reform of company law, not to piecemeal reform but to the elaboration of a new law to replace the law of 1867 in its entirety. The bill that emerged aimed at preventing the abuses that had appeared since 1867, particularly those associated with the recent boom and crash. This involved adding safeguards at the time of the founding of SAs and CPAs, and adding

29 Ibid., 11 Mar. 1882, pp. 287-90.
30 F¹²6833ᴬ, CCP to Min. of Commerce, 23 May 1883.

an array of civil and criminal penalties for infraction of the formalities of foundation. The committee worked long and arduously, producing a bill of 108 articles, as compared with the 67 articles that sufficed for the law of 1867, only finishing its work eleven months later on 21 February 1883.[31]

The provisions of the bill incorporated many of the suggestions that the critics of the law of 1867 had raised. No bearer shares could be issued until the shares were completely paid up. Specific mention was required in all publicity and on the subscription form of the portion of the capital in fixed assets, and the portion in cash to come from the issue of shares. Upon the request of one-quarter of the stockholders at the time of a company's founding, the fixed assets would be appraised by experts appointed by the president of a commercial tribunal. Companies were forbidden to purchase their own shares, except under clearly defined conditions, a provision intended to prevent companies from speculating in their own shares. The bill specifically recognized the right of bondholders to act collectively to protect their interests. An official publication was to be established to provide the public with more information on companies. And foreign corporations operating in France were to be subjected to the same restrictions as French companies.

Although the committee's bill gave general satisfaction to the critics of the law of 1867, predictably, the bill was anathema to liberals and to sections of the business community. A most influential critique came from Pierre Mathieu-Bodet, a former Minister of Finance, who doubted if a good law could emerge in the atmosphere created by the crash.[32] He claimed the bill was overly restrictive, multiplying as it did the number of acts of omission and commission when a company was founded that could result in the company being declared null, and the number of instances where directors, and commissioners charged with verifying the accounts, could be held pecuniarily liable by the courts. Mathieu-Bodet listed 26 different acts, or omissions of action, which could result in the company being declared null, and provided a long list of fines and prison sentences that could be levied against company officers for infractions, many of them simply involving negligence rather than any criminal intent. He was also critical of the provisions that would subject foreign companies, operating in France, to the same restrictions as French companies. Finally, he expressed the hope that the legislature would liberalize the bill.

---

31 Altogether the commission held 49 meetings, 43 of which were devoted to the elaboration of the bill on joint-stock companies. The *procès-verbaux* of the commission is in AN C5514. Also L. Arnault, *Rapport de la Commission extra-parlementaire du 14 fevrier 1882 à l'appui d'un projet de loi sur les sociétés* (Paris, 1884); *Journal officiel*, Senat, Doc. parlem., Jan. 1884, annexe No. 72, pp. 1097-1113, contains the text of the bill.

32 *Observations sur le projet de loi relatif à la réforme de la législation sur les sociétés.* Offprint from the *Journal des économistes* (15 May 1884).

Paul Leroy-Beaulieu and Alfred Neymarck were more moderate in their criticism of the bill. Like Mathieu-Bodet, both criticized the provisions aimed at making directors liable.[33] Since no serious and wealthy man would accept to become a director, according to Leroy-Beaulieu, the posts would be taken over by straw men and adventurers with nothing to lose. Both argued in favor of abandoning the fetishism of the minimum 500 francs share for companies with a capital of more than 200,000 francs. Leroy-Beaulieu would also allow the introduction into France of the English preferred share (*action de priorité*). Neymarck proposed to leave the size of reserve funds to each company's discretion. Both approved of some of the bill's innovations: Neymarck welcomed the provision that would establish an official publication, which would contain the by-laws of the newly founded companies and other pertinent information. In some cases the law did not go far enough: Neymarck thought the widespread practice of issuing bonds while a company still had part of their shares uncalled, should be prohibited.

The bill was first introduced into the Senate in December 1883, probably as a gesture to Senator J. F. J. Bozérian, who had presided over the extraparliamentary commission. Bozérian was also the president of the Senate's committee that examined the bill.[34] He later served as floor manager (*rapporteur*) of the bill during the Senate's debates in October and November 1884. The debate in the Senate was long, but generally confined to the technicalities rather than the principles of the law. Bozérian, a former avocat à la Court de Cassation was the veritable father of the bill, which easily passed the Senate on 29 November 1884 with no significant changes.

The Senate's bill met with a barrage of criticism similar to that which greeted the government's bill, not surprising in view of their similarity. But among members of the legal profession the bill had its supporters. A. Vavasseur, a member of the extraparliamentary commission, gave a favorable analysis of the bill in the pages of the *Revue des Sociétés*, which he edited.[35] Like others, however, he was critical of the large number of instances in which a company could be declared null, if certain formalities were not observed during its foundation. The penalties were exorbitant in view of the minor importance of some of the formalities. Vavasseur also regretted the omission of a requirement that all fixed assets should be appraised by a court-appointed official, a provision that would hinder the founding of many companies.

---

[33] P. Leroy-Beaulieu, *Economiste français*, 13 Dec. 1884, pp. 725-28; P. Neymarck, *Rapport sur les réformes de la loi de 1867 sur les sociétés* (Paris, 1882).

[34] The members of the Senate committee were Alfred Naquet, Eymard-Duvernay, Jean-Jules Clamageran, A. J. A. Ronjat, Charles Auguste Merlin, Esquirrou de Parieu, Malens, and Eugène Gouin.

[35] *Revue des Sociétés*, III (1885), pp. 51-57, 105-10, 218-26, 306-12 and 367-70.

For E. E. Thaller of the law faculty of Lyon, an admirer of the stringencies of German company law, the bill was, if anything, insufficiently restrictive.[36] Since many of the remedies against fraud were, in Thaller's view, likely to be ineffective, he proposed that all new companies be subjected to a final review by the courts to certify that all the formalities of the law had been observed. However, as time passed, the enthusiasm for restrictions generated by the crash of 1882 waned.

Second Thoughts

More than a year elapsed between the vote of the Senate and the introduction of the bill into the Chamber. In January 1886, the bill was referred to a committee of the Chamber headed by Maurice Rouvier. Meanwhile, the government solicited the opinions of all the chambers of commerce, commercial tribunals, and the higher courts on the bill, and conflicting opinions continued to emanate from the financial press.[37] One of the most influential critiques was that of Antoine Jacquand, a lawyer and businessman, and a former president of the chamber of commerce of Lyon.[38] Jacquand, a champion of liberty as opposed to those who saw only "wolves and sheep,"[39] directed his heaviest criticism, as had many others, against the large number of instances which could result in a company's being declared null, and against the pecuniary liabilities and special criminal penalties that could be incurred by founders and members of boards of directors. The effect of such a law would be to "drive savings into foreign securities . . . while our large financial and industrial enterprises became the prey of adventurers who offered no guarantees other than their audacity and effrontery."[40] For Jacquand, joint-stock companies were no more risky than proprietorships, though their failures were, he admitted, more serious.

Responses from the chambers of commerce were numerous and, in many cases, it was obvious that the bill was considered with great care.[41] Most of the responses were generally favorable, but the important chambers of Lyon, Toulouse, Marseille and Reims were adversely critical.[42] The influen-

---

[36] *De la réforme de la loi sur les sociétés par actions* (Paris, 1886), which appeared originally in the *Journal des sociétés civiles et commerciales* in 1884, 1885 and 1886.

[37] Paul Leroy-Beaulieu was critical: *Economiste français*, 23 Jan. 1886, pp. 97-99, while Alfred Neymarck described the bill as "excellent" in *Le Rentier* in January 1886, *Finances contemporaines*, I, p. 225.

[38] *Examen critique du projet de loi sur les sociétés par actions* (Paris, 1886).

[39] Ibid., p. 15.

[40] Ibid., p. 22.

[41] These responses are in $F^{12}6833^B$ and C 5426.

[42] Ibid. and Jacquand, *Examen critique du projet de loi*, pp. 34-38.

tial Chamber of Commerce of Paris was generally favorable,[43] as were two reports from the Court of Cassation,[44] though some courts had substantial reservations, particularly concerning what they regarded as excessively harsh penal provisions.[45]

The adverse criticism was not without effect. In the Chamber of Deputies, only one member of the Chamber's committee favored the bill in the form passed by the Senate.[46] Yves Guyot, a member of the committee, wished the new law to deal only with questions of registration and disclosure.[47] A majority of the members favored reducing the number of cases that could result in declaring the company null. René Brice, a member of the committee, offered a substitute bill in 1886 based on these suggestions.[48] In 1888, François-Marie Thévenet went further, offering a bill of only four articles, abrogating the law of 1867 and other special legislation governing joint-stock companies, establishing complete freedom for enterprise subject only to the common law, except for disclosure requirements.[49] This radical proposal had no more chance than the Senate's bill, but clearly the tide was running against the restrictionists. The elections of 1889 brought the legislature to an end before the committee took any action. It is likely that the divergence of opinion on the committee prevented any consensus on a bill.

Just before the elections of 1889, the movement for liberalization received a setback with the failure of de Lesseps' Panama Canal Company and the collapse of Secretan's attempt to corner the world's copper market, which brought down not only the Société Industrielle et Commerciale des Métaux, but the Comptoir d'Escompte, a blue chip pillar of the financial community. To many these latest casualties again pinpointed certain weaknesses in company law, and dramatically illustrated the need for restrictive legislation. The fall of the Panama Company was expected, but that of the supposedly strong Comptoir d'Escompte came with surprising suddenness. In contrast to 1882, when the government did little to halt the debacle, even exhibiting what to some seemed like unseemly haste in precipitating the demise of the Union Générale, in 1889 Maurice Rouvier, the Minister of Finance, led a successful rescue operation to limit the effects of the collapse of one of the major deposit banks.

---

[43] Avis du 23 mai 1882 and 1 avril 1885, somewhat modified by that of 9 fev. 1888. See *Revue des sociétés*, VI (1888), pp. 283-85.

[44] *Revue des sociétés*, IV (1886), pp. 353-55, 408-14, 542-44, 606-13 and also in C 5426.

[45] For example, the Tribunals de Commerce of Rouen and Havre and the Cours d'appel of Lyon and Toulouse, C 5426.

[46] *Revue des sociétés*, V (1887), p. 410; C 5426.

[47] Ibid.

[48] *Journal officiel*, Chambre, Doc. parlem., annexe de la séance du 14 oct. 1886 for the text. Brice, a prominent businessman, cited the deliberations of the CC de Lyon many times.

[49] *Revue des sociétés*, VI (1888), p. 170; for the *exposé des motifs*, see ibid., pp. 281-83.

Denfert Rochereau, the director of the Comptoir d'Escompte unwisely involved the bank in Eugène Secretan's scheme to corner the copper market in 1887-1889.[50] Secretan, headed the Société Industrielle et Commerciale des Métaux, which had been created in 1881 by the merger of his own Société Métallurgique du Cuivre and the Société J.-J. Laveissière et fils. The new company, capitalized at 25 MF, immediately issued 20 MF of bonds to procure working capital. Unlike many creations of the boom of the early 1880s, the SICM survived and, for a time, prospered.

World copper production in the mid-1880s amounted to a little more than 200,000 tons annually, selling for about 1,000 francs a ton. Secretan believed that if most of the copper available in market inventories, and most current production could be controlled, then substantial profits could be realized. The sums required to achieve this control were enormous, substantially more than Secretan realized. In 1887, Secretan took the lead in putting together a syndicate, which concluded agreements with many of the major mining companies to purchase their entire output for three years, guaranteeing a price of 1,700 to 1,750 francs (£68 to £70 a ton), about 70% above the going market price. Further funds were raised with the doubling of the capital of the SICM to 50 MF in March 1888, the public offering of the new shares being issued at 750 francs, a premium of 250 francs.

The syndicate was replaced by the creation of a private company, the Compagnie Auxiliaire des Métaux, whose shares were not offered to the public. Capitalized at 40 MF, divided into shares of 5,000 francs, CAM's 8,000 shares were subscribed by both institutions and individuals. The SICM subscribed 4,715 shares and the Comptoir d'Escompte 1,000. Various members of the board of directors of SICM (Secretan, Denfert-Rochereau, Arbel, Joubert and Hentsch took 1,153 shares on their own account, Hentsch alone subscribing to 428 shares). The remaining shares were taken by the Banque de Paris (300), private bankers, and others, mainly in Paris and Switzerland; diverse Swiss investors accounted for 420 shares.

When the resources of the SICM and the CAM proved insufficient, Denfert-Rochereau used funds of the Comptoir d'Escompte. In addition, the Comptoir d'Escompte guaranteed the contracts passed between the syndicate and the copper mining companies. The collapse occurred early in March of 1889. Like other attempts before and since, the corner proved to be elusive. As the price of copper rose, more of the metal miraculously appeared on the market from inventories and stockpiles, and perhaps from

50 The following account of the corner is based primarily upon Arthur Raffalovich, "L'Accaparement des cuivres et l'effondrement du Comptoir d'Escompte," *L'Année économique, 1888-1889*, pp. 193-215. See also, Edmond Théry, *Faits et chiffres, questions économiques d'actualité* (Paris, 1889), pp. 187-208; A. Neymarck, *Finances contemporaines*, VI, pp. 299-312.

mining companies violating their exclusive agreements with the syndicate. And the normal demand for copper dried up as the price tripled. Much more copper was available than Secretan and Denfert-Rochereau imagined. Altogether, the Comptoir advanced over 145 MF to the SICM, which was guaranteed by approximately 68,000 tons of copper. Denfert-Rochereau watched the developments with growing apprehension, eventually realizing that the game was lost. Rumors concerning the solidity of SICM and the Comptoir d'Escompte caused their shares to decline on the Bourse. On the 5th of March, Denfert-Rochereau committed suicide. The 6th of March was "black Wednesday" with panic selling of the shares of both SICM and the Comptoir. The panic was not confined to these two institutions. Copper mining stocks (*e.g.* Rio Tinto) which had risen on the higher price of copper, fell. Paul Leroy-Beaulieu estimated the loss in copper company shares at 80 to 100 MF.[51]

To avert a general banking crisis, Minister of Finance Maurice Rouvier met with the important bankers of Paris on the evening of March 7th to find a way to save the Comptoir d'Escompte. It was agreed that the Bank of France would advance 100 MF, of which the first 20 MF would be guaranteed by the major public and private banks of the city. Rothschild frères led the list with 3 MF, followed by Paribas with 2.5 MF. The directors of the Comptoir d'Escompte were forced to pledge 2.5 MF of their own money. Later in the month a second operation for 40 MF was necessary, half of which was guaranteed by bankers, industrialists, and brokers.

To protect the bank's depositors, a new Comptoir Nationale d'Escompte, capitalized at 40 MF, was immediately founded to replace the old one. Liquidating the old Comptoir also conveniently relieved the new Comptoir of the contractual obligation to buy the output of major copper companies at an inflated price. Copper fell to its pre-corner price and the liquidation of the copper stocks brought only about 68 MF. Eventual losses from the liquidation of the Comptoir totaled about 80 MF, which were borne by the Comptoir's shareholders. The timely intervention of Rouvier and the Bank of France averted what might have become a serious financial crisis.[52]

These events undoubtedly tempered the enthusiasm for liberal reform in both the Chamber and in the International Congress on Corporations that gathered later in the year as part of the festivities connected with the Paris Exposition of 1889 to mark the centennial of the Revolution. The Congress brought together professors, lawyers, public officials, financial journalists and businessmen to discuss needed reforms in corporate law, the problems

---

[51] A. Raffalovich, "L'Accaparement des cuivres," p. 205.

[52] The same scenario was played out a few years later following the equally unexpected fall of another important bank, the Société de Depôts et de Comptes Courants. See A. Neymarck, *Finances contemporaines*, VI, pp. 343-54.

of multinational corporations, and to promote greater international uniformity in corporate law. The Congress adopted 30 resolutions toward these ends. Even though only a small number of the delegates were businessmen, who took an even smaller part in the proceedings as compared with professors and lawyers, professions more accustomed to expressing themselves in public, the resolutions of the Congress were indicative of the prevailing mood in regard to company law.[53]

The mood was cautious, though far from an acceptance of the ultra-restrictive proposals produced earlier in the decade. On the restrictive side, the Congress voted resolutions that provided: Payments on subscribed shares had to be deposited in an officially designated bank; the fixed assets of a company had to be appraised by a court-appointed expert before the company could be founded; bearer shares had to be completely paid-up, and for shares where only a portion was called, the original subscribers were to be liable for future calls, even if they had sold their shares, for a certain period (the resolution mentioned two years). The Congress also favored restrictions on the issue of additional shares: No new shares could be issued below par; if issued above par, the premium was to go into the company's reserve fund; no new shares could be issued unless the calls were completely paid on the old shares.

On the liberal side, the Congress resolved that a company should not be declared null simply because of the violation of some of the legal formalities at the time of its founding. Instead, these violations should result in the civil and criminal liability of promoters and directors. The existence of founders' shares (*parts de fondateur*) should be recognized by statute, and defined only to confer a right to profits, and to exclude any right to the company's capital. The use of preferred shares should also be permitted. There were also a number of resolutions likely to command the support of both restrictionists and liberals: Company charters were to be published in an official journal and must appear before the subscription of shares; all SAs and CPAs were to be considered as commercial, thus bringing all companies under the commercial jurisdiction and ending the anomaly of some companies, such as coal mines, falling within the civil jurisdiction; stockholders should have the right to convoke a stockholders' meeting, and bondholders should have the right to attend stockholders' meetings and the right to be heard there. These resolutions offered a program for reform, and many of them became law over the next 25 years.

Fears that restrictive legislation would be passed reappeared in 1890 when a new committee of the Chamber began to consider the Senate's bill.

---

[53] Congrès International des sociétés par Actions, 1889. *Compte Rendu* (Paris, 1890), pp. 311-18.

Two prominent businessmen, Jacques Siegfried and Raphaël G. Lévy, renewed the attack on the Senate's bill and its "arsenal of penalties." They counted 41 conditions and formalities that had to be fulfilled when a company was founded, the omission of a single one of which would result in the nullification of the company *de plein droit* and would subject the founders and board members to an array of civil and criminal penalties. An error in the list of share subscriptions, or publishing certain documents on the ninth, rather than the tenth day before the formation of a company, could result in its being declared null after the company had been operating for many years.[54] "The bill does not say that the judge may declare the company null; it says he must do so."[55]

Siegfried repeated his attack on the bill at a discussion of the Société d'Economie Politique in April 1890.[56] He compared the rigors of actual and proposed legislation in France with the more liberal law of other countries, asking the members of the Society "to raise a cry of alarm, because the enactment of the bill would be disastrous."[57] Arthur Raffalovich warned that all founders and board members would be henceforth "straw men" if the bill were passed, because serious reputable men would decline such positions. André Sabatier expressed the view that only a few changes in the 1867 law were necessary. Not all would go as far as Siegfried in liberalizing the law. Adolphe Coste did not wish to leave the punishment of illegal acts of founders and board members solely to Article 405 of the Penal Code.[58]

The fears about the passage of the Senate's bill proved to be unfounded. As with the 1886 committee, most of the members of the new committee were opposed to the Senate's bill.[59] The new Minister of Justice was no other than F. M. Thévenet who had only two years earlier proposed a radical clearing of the statute books on company law. Thévenet encouraged the committee to liberalize the bill, even suggesting that company charters, like other contracts, should be regulated by the common law (*principes généraux du droit*).[60] The committee began its task of revising the Senate's bill, and by the end of June had worked its way through the first 74 articles of the bill; all in vain, as the task was never resumed. The committee apparently did not meet at all in 1891, and when it met in February 1892, it was to consider two bills offered by members of the Chamber. At that time, the committee

[54] J. Siegfried and R. G. Levy, *Du Relèvement du marché financier français* (Paris, 1890), p. 64.

[55] Ibid.

[56] *Economiste français*, 12 April 1890, p. 457.

[57] Ibid.

[58] Ibid., pp. 457-58.

[59] PV of the committee, séance du 5 fév. 1890, C 5514. Only two members of the committee (A. B. Brugnot and Comte Anatole Lemercier) favored the Senate's bill.

[60] *Revue des sociétés*, VIII (1890), p. 214.

decided to propose a limited reform rather than return to the task of revising the Senate's bill.[61] The end of the legislature was too near to allow sufficient time for the completion and passage of a bill modifying company law.

The Law of 1893

The short bill that emerged, with some revisions in the Senate, became the law of 1 August 1893.[62] The law, which dealt with some of the more pressing problems, contained both liberal and restrictive provisions. It lowered the minimum value of shares from 500 francs to 100 francs for corporations with a capitalization of over 200,000 francs and from 100 to 25 francs for those companies capitalized at 200,000 francs or less. The bill that passed the Chamber provided for shares of 25 francs minimum for all companies irrespective of their capitalization, but the Senate adopted the higher figure for larger companies. However, on all shares of less than 100 francs, the entire amount had to be paid-in rather than the usual one-quarter. The calling of a minimum of one-quarter was retained for shares of 100 francs or more. The law tightened the provisions for bearer shares by requiring that they must be entirely paid-up, rather than the minimum of one-half required by the law of 1867. This provision was to make it possible to locate shareholders with unpaid calls in the event of bankruptcy. Original subscribers or buyers of shares could be liable for all unpaid calls for two years, even if they sold their shares. The Senate added a provision prohibiting the negotiation for two years of shares attributed to founders in exchange for fixed assets. These provisions were an attempt to prevent founders and speculators from abandoning the company at an early stage by unloading their shares on the public.

The new law afforded some satisfaction to the many criticisms concerning the grounds on which a company could be declared null under existing law. Nullity forced the liquidation of the company and subjected founders and board members to civil and criminal suits from stockholders and third parties. If the cause of the nullity had been remedied, or was in the process of being remedied, the suit was inadmissible. The time during which such actions could be filed was limited, and judges were given greater discretionary power so that they were not required to declare a company null for

[61] C 5514, PV, séance du 26 fév. 1892.

[62] J. B. Sirey, *Recueil général des lois et des arrêts, Année 1893*, pp. 569-77; A. Vavasseur, *Commentaire de la loi du 1er août 1893 sur les sociétés par actions* (Paris, 1894); and the report of Claude Chausel de Coussergues, *Journal officiel*, 10 April 1893, Débats parlem., p. 531, text in *Journal officiel*, Doc. parlem., Sept. 1892, p. 970.

minor infractions. This greatly reduced the risks run by founders and board members.

The new law also subjected civil companies using the joint-stock form of organization to commercial law, thus changing the distinction between civil and commercial companies from their **object** to their **form**. The practical import of this change meant that civil companies would fall under commercial law in the event of liquidation, which was cheaper, faster and more equitable than the civil law; the recent liquidation of the Panama Canal Company, a civil society, afforded ample evidence of the disadvantages. These companies would also be subjected to more rigorous accounting and disclosure requirements, and their founders and board members would come under the provisions — civil and penal liabilities — of the law of 1867. The most important category of civil companies using the commercial form were coal mines, which because of certain anomalies in French law, traceable to making the operation of a coal mine compatible with a title of nobility, could be formed as civil companies. The law passed with little debate, most of which occurred in the Senate and involved legal technicalities rather than the general principles of company law. No further reform in company law occurred for almost a decade, but within two years a controversy arose over legalizing 25 francs shares for all companies.

Gold Stock Fever, 1895-1896

On 26 October 1895, Georges Graux, joined by Jules Méline, C. C. A. Jonnart, and L. C. F. Boudenoot, introduced into the Chamber a bill to permit the issue of 25 francs shares in France. Under the law of 1893, these shares could be issued only by companies whose capital was less than 200,000 francs. Graux had proposed a bill in 1891 to allow shares of 50 francs, and the Chamber's original version of the 1893 law permitted 25 francs shares. In 1891, Graux's justification of the bill was to promote social peace by providing workers with the opportunity to buy shares: "When the day comes in a coal mining company employing 1,500 workers in which 1,200 are stockholders, the doctrine of participation in profits will have become a reality."[63]

In 1895, the 25 francs share received additional support because of the massive invasion of £1 par value gold mining shares issued by English companies. Since 25 francs shares were illegal in France (except for small companies), they could not be quoted on the Paris Bourse, nor traded by the official brokers of the Parquet. They were introduced into France by the

---

[63] Quoted in *Journal officiel*, Chambre, Doc. parlem., Oct. 1895, p. 1430.

technically illegal, but necessary and tolerated, Coulisse. Hence they escaped being examined by the committee of the Bourse which determined if a company's shares could be quoted. This examination, at least, offered some minimum guarantees that the company possessed some substance. In the gold share mania of 1894-1895, Graux estimated that from 1.2 to 1.5 billion francs worth of shares were bought by French speculators. Not only were these shares highly speculative, but the French treasury suffered because these shares escaped both the transmission tax, since they were not quoted on the Bourse, and the dividend tax. A 25 francs gold mining share cost a French speculator about 27F 50c, including 1F 87c (one shilling 6 pence) for the English stamp, which on an estimated 6 million shares, an estimate that in Graux's opinion was too low, produced 11.2 MF for the English treasury; the French government received only 3.18 MF in stamp duties.[64] Graux further argued that the 25 francs share would stimulate French commerce and industry.

The support of Méline could be expected to rally conservatives, protectionists and nationalists, while liberals could be expected to support any amelioration in the rigors of company law. It appeared that the bill had sufficient support for passage. With the bill designated as "urgent," a committee of the Chamber under the presidency of Graux began to examine the bill toward the end of 1895. A majority of the members of the committee favored the bill and on 7 February 1896, the Minister of Finance gave his blessing; better the money should go to domestic enterprise than foreign. On 14 February 1896, the head of the official brokers (*Syndic du Compagnie des Agents de Change*), de Vermeuil, enthusiastically endorsed the bill "given the fact that about a billion francs worth of these securities have been introduced already on the French market in contravention of the law."[65] De Vermeuil did not say how much this cost the official brokers in lost commissions. The public, de Vermeuil averred, wanted the 25 francs share, and his parting words to the committee were "above all, I repeat, let us make haste."[66] In addition, the committee interviewed two members of the Coulisse, Lange and Waubert, and six bankers. Lange estimated the value of 25 francs shares held in France to be about 1.5 billion francs, and that one-half of the gold mining shares for which the Coulisse was the intermediary were purchased by the official brokers of the Parquet for their customers. Claim-

[64] Exposé des motifs, *Journal officiel*, Chambre, Doc. parlem., 1895, No. 1579.

[65] C 5612, Dossier 3268.

[66] C 5612, Dossier 3628. De Vermeuil reported that the coulisse did not negotiate all the gold mining shares purchased by French citizens. For some companies (he cited Modderfontein) the shares were only negotiated in London; he estimated that French capital in Modderfontein accounted for 80% of the total. At least one member of the committee, Goiraud, thought gold stocks a good investment, estimating returns from the Transvaal in 1895 to have been about 200 MF.

ing to be always partisans of freedom, the representatives of the Coulisse added their support to the 25 francs share.

The bankers were divided: J. H. Thors, a general manager (*directeur*) of Paribas, Baron Hély d'Oissel, chairman of the board of the Société Générale, and Adrien Mazerat, a member of the board of the Crédit Lyonnais favored the 25 francs share. Hély d'Oissel thought that channeling the savings of French workers into industrial enterprise was highly desirable; he also blamed the 2 francs registration fee on every share for pushing the French to invest in foreign companies. For Thors, the 25 francs share had already proved itself and legalizing it would permit the guarantees offered by official listing on the Bourse. Mazerat was reluctant, "but given present conditions, I think the surveillance of the Parquet is preferable to none at all.[67]

Emile Mercet, vice-chairman of the board of the Comptoir d'Escompte and Alexis Rostand, a member of the board of the same bank, were resolutely opposed to the 25 francs share as encouraging dangerous speculation, though Mercet recognized that the law would pass in spite of his advice. De Montplanet, the chairman of the board of the Crédit Industriel et Commercial, also opposed the introduction of the 25 francs share because it would encourage speculation. He argued that the 100 francs share was sufficient for all needs, even those of workers. The real reason behind the bill was to remove the obstacles to the circulation of gold mining shares. For de Montplanet,

... it would be better to reform company law, whose draconian provisions, further aggravated by the courts, do not permit an honest man who is concerned about his honor to found an enterprise, obliging him to have recourse to straw men. In this respect, something could be done to retain French capital and prevent it from emigrating to England where English law offers enormous advantages.[68]

On the other questions in which the committee was interested, the witnesses all agreed that the 25 francs share should be completely paid-up. (If only one-quarter were called, as in the case of the 100 francs share, the shares could be negotiated for as little as 6F 25c.) However they were divided on whether or not these shares should be allowed to be quoted on the futures' market (*marché à terme*). The testimony also brought to light some interesting differences between the London Exchange and the Paris Bourse. Small transactions for one or two shares, which were common in Paris, were rare in London where shares were more likely to be exchanged in packets of 2,000 (though the English shares were of smaller denomina-

---

67 C 5612, Dossier 3268.
68 C 5612, Dossier 3268.

tion). Hély d'Oissel alleged that English speculators attempted to float shares on the French market at a high premium, then worked to depress them before repurchasing them. The committee put the finishing touches on the bill early in March; it was reported to the Chamber in June but it never reached the floor of the Chamber, though not because, as Emmanuel Vidal was later to claim, "to tell the truth, that document was of such little substance that it could not have survived the first words of an open debate."[69]

Outside the Chamber, the bill was criticized both by Vidal, the editor of the financial journal *Cote de la Bourse et de la Banque* and by Dervillé, the president of the Tribunal of Commerce of Paris.[70] Dervillé noted that the 25 francs share was not an effective remedy to the much discussed "stagnation of enterprise." Even as the committee met, the boom in gold mining shares had given way, inevitably, to the bust, which carried away a large number of English companies, cooled the ardor of French speculators for the 25 francs share, and highlighted the dangers of unbridled speculation.[71] This change in the market rendered the bill unnecessary. The worries over the "stagnation of enterprise" were transitory. Within a few years the big domestic boom of the turn of the century was underway, which by comparison with the earlier 1879-1881 boom, was smaller but healthier, and less chaotic on the down side. The new boom marked the opening of a new era of growth for the corporate form of business organization. Corporations were becoming larger and more numerous; publicists of all political shades discovered and agonized over what appeared to be increasing concentration of economic power; and predictably, the law of 1867 remained a focal point of controversy.

The Reform Agenda, 1898-1914

In 1898, the Ministry of Commerce appointed Rodolphe Rousseau, a lawyer and an expert in corporate law, to investigate why so many French companies were incorporating under Belgian and English law. What was wrong with the French corporation? After a comparative analysis of French,

---

69 Emmanuel Vidal, *The History and Methods of the Paris Bourse* (Washington, D. C., 1910), p. 232. See *Journal officiel*, Chambre, Doc. parlem., June 1896, annexe no. 1950 for the text of the bill.

70 For the lawyers the 25 francs share invoked the specter of John Law and the rue Quincampoix, *e.g.* A. Vavasseur, *Revue des sociétés*, Feb. 1896, reprinted in *Sociétés, syndicats, associations*, II, pp. 726-27.

71 R. Nouel, *Les Sociétés par actions, la réforme* (Paris, 1911), pp. 93-94. Nouel attributed the stagnation to the loss of confidence in SPAs since the Crash of 1882, a view which greatly exaggerates the role of the SPA.

Belgian and English corporate law, Rousseau concluded that English and Belgian laws were more liberal, offering advantages not to be found in France. Rousseau suggested certain changes in French law, most of which were to appear on the agenda of the Second International Congress on Corporations held in Paris in 1900, for which Rousseau served as secretary (*rapporteur*). His proposals also figured prominently among the reforms proposed by the Extraparliamentary Committee of 1902, for which he also served as secretary. Rousseau's report to the Minister of Commerce, and his subsequent advocacy of liberal reform, aimed at ending unnecessary restrictions and provided for fuller disclosure and access to vital information regarding corporations.

Rousseau singled out the high cost of founding a corporation in France, as compared with England and Belgium, as the most important reason for French companies to incorporate outside of France. Other foreigners, in addition to the French, founded companies in Belgium. In 1896, 60 companies were incorporated under Belgian law by foreigners to operate outside of Belgium, of which 20 were French; in 1897 there were 72 such companies, of which 30 were French.[72] Costs for founding a company in England were less than one-half of those for France, and incorporation was even cheaper in Belgium.[73]

Neither English nor Belgian law established a minimum value for shares. Rousseau proposed adopting the fully called 25 francs shares in France, a reform that had already been pushed for various reasons by others in the 1890s. He advocated removing the two year inalienability of shares representing fixed assets, or shares representing the expenses of founding the company (*actions d'apport*), which the 1893 law established when the Senate, in a conservative reflex, amended the Chamber's bill. The inalienability of these *apport* shares was another reason why promoters resorted to Belgian law.[74] Rousseau also proposed to abandon the system of verification of non-pecuniary assets to be exchanged for stock required by the law of 1867, on the grounds that the verification was "absolutely illusory."[75] Under the 1867 law, a commissioner, who was in fact chosen by the founders, reported to the founding meeting of stockholders on the evaluation of fixed assets and other costs to be compensated for by stock in the new company. The exaggeration of the value of these assets and costs constituted a continuous source of high profits to company promoters bordering on, or in fact, fraud. Never, according to Rousseau, had the

---

[72] R. Rousseau, "Rapport à le ministre du commerce," October 1898, published in *Congrès international des sociétés par actions, 1900* (Paris, 1900), pp. 397-463.

[73] Ibid., pp. 424-25.

[74] John P. McKay, *Pioneers for Profit*, p. 207.

[75] R. Rousseau, "Rapport," p. 433.

founding of a company been hindered by an unfavorable report from the commissioner for verification.[76] This illusory guarantee did not exist in England or Belgium. Rousseau explicitly rejected the German system of having an officially appointed outside expert, though many French legists favored this system.

Rousseau found the English and Belgian law on disclosure and publicity superior to that of France. In England, incorporation is preceded by issuing a detailed prospectus, and in Belgium a draft company charter is published before the founding of the company. Rousseau proposed that company charters be published before shares were subscribed. He also proposed to establish an official journal for the publication of company charters, which would also contain news of appointments and resignations of board members, and financial statements, imitating the Belgian supplement to the official *Moniteur*. This proposal had been bouncing around in France for 25 years. In 1889, the International Congress on Corporations adopted a resolution favoring the establishment of such a publication.

Rousseau proposed to abolish the restrictions that prevented the issue of preferred shares in France, shares which proved so useful in England. Copying Belgian practice, he advanced an easier method of amending corporate charters by stockholders' meetings.[77] Further, a certain number of shareholders should have the power to employ the services of an accounting expert to verify the company's financial statements, and also a certain number of shareholders should have the power to convene a special shareholders' meeting, both of which were approved by resolutions of the 1889 Congress on Corporations. The most important reasons French promoters went elsewhere were lower costs, the ability to issue 25 francs shares, and the immediate negotiability of shares representing non-pecuniary assets. The rest of Rousseau's proposed reforms had little bearing upon why company promoters went elsewhere, but these important planks in the liberal program could be justified by practice elsewhere, particularly in Belgium. Rousseau's report furnished an agenda for the reform movement over the next fifteen years, a movement in which he continued to play a leading role.

The Paris Exposition of 1900 to welcome the new century played host to 127 international congresses, one of which was the Second International Congress on Corporations, presided over by the distinguished French legist Charles Lyon-Caen, and with Rodolphe Rousseau as secretary. Like its

---

[76] Ibid.

[77] French law required that to amend the charter, one-half of the shares must be represented at the stockholders' meeting, a proportion that was difficult to attain for large companies whose shares were widely held. Rousseau proposed the Belgian practice of then calling a second stockholders' meeting, this one possessing the power to amend the charter no matter how many shares were represented.

predecessor of 1889, most of those attending were French, with lawyers, professors of law and bankers predominating. The tenor of the 1900 Congress was distinctly more liberal than its predecessor eleven years earlier. The reform proposals contained in Rousseau's report to the Minister of Commerce were on the agenda for discussion by the Congress. Rousseau played a prominent part in the discussions of the Congress and most of the reforms he advocated were embodied in resolutions approved by the Congress, pointing the way for the reform of French law. The Congress approved a resolution to repeal the provision of the 1893 law that made shares not representing cash subscriptions inalienable for two years. The inalienability of these shares was particularly inconvenient in certain circumstances, for example, when a proprietor wanted to convert his enterprise into a corporation in order to retire, or protect the family patrimony. The shares he received for the firm were tied up for two years in a new company over which he may have relinquished control. The courts also invoked this provision in mergers of two firms, with the result that most of the shares of the successor firm were immobilized for two years.[78]

What was not said was that there were legal ways to circumvent the provisions of the 1893 law regarding the inalienability of these shares. For example, in 1897 the Société Métallurgique de Champigneulles et Neuves-Maisons merged with Chatillon-Commentry, the shareholders of Champigneulles Neuves-Maisons receiving two shares of Chatillon-Commentry for one of theirs. When the stockholders Champigneulles Neuves-Maisons voted on the merger, they were told that the new shares, in compliance with the 1893 law, could not be delivered for two years. However, those with registered shares could sell them (under civil law) by a notorial act or by private agreement (*sous seing privé*) with notification to the Chatillon-Commentry Company so that the shares would eventually be delivered to the proper party. Those with bearer shares had no such problem since they could be passed from hand to hand.[79] Although this method had its inconveniences, it certainly violated the spirit of Article 2 of the 1893 law. The Congress recognized that one reason founders' shares became popular was to circumvent this provision of the 1893 law.[80]

Though founders' shares had been issued before 1893, it was only after the restrictions on shares received in exchange for non-pecuniary assets in 1893 that they became common. By 1914, almost all new corporations selling shares to the public created founders' shares to reward promoters for ideas, time, effort and expenses, which enabled them to profit if the enter-

---

[78] Congrès International des sociétés par actions, 1900, *Compte rendu* (Paris, 1900), p. 111.

[79] 65AQ K46[1], Report to stockholders of Champigneulles Neuves-Maisons on the proposed merger.

[80] Congrès, 1900, *Compte rendu* (Paris, 1900), pp. 108-9 and 119.

prise succeeded, and, since they were immediately negotiable, often enabled them to reap handsome sums even if the enterprise failed to survive. The first notable creation of founders' shares, perhaps their origin as some claim, was by the Suez Canal Company, which issued 100 *parts de fondateur* in remuneration for preliminary expenses before the company was founded. These shares, which entitled their holders to 10% of net profits, proved to be immensely profitable. Founders' shares were also issued by the Panama Company, initially selling at 5,000 francs, reaching 30,000 francs each at their apogee, before eventually falling to nothing.[81] The holders of the old shares in the bankrupt Comptoir d'Escompte in 1889 were compensated by 60,000 *parts de fondateur* in the new Comptoir National d'Escompte. Founders' shares were sometimes given to initial subscribers of shares, or to those subscribing a certain number of shares.

A typical provision regarding founders' shares is to be found in the by-laws of the SA created in 1875 to take over the concession of providing gas to the city of Bordeaux. Original subscribers of the 6,000 shares of the Compagnie du Gaz de Bordeaux received one founders' share for every 20 shares they subscribed. These founders' shares were entitled to a share of the net profits of the enterprise after: (1) 5% had been paid into the company's legal reserve in accordance with the provisions of the law of 1867; (2) a levy to provide for the amortization of the company's shares before the expiration of its concession in 1904; (3) 5% to the stockholders on the paid-in amount of the company's shares; and (4) 10% to the members of the board of directors. The remaining amount (if any) would be divided with 75% going to the shareholders and 25% to the 300 founders' shares.[82] Founders' shares did not represent equity in the corporation and were not entitled to any share of the capital in the event of dissolution. They were negotiable and gave their owners the right to a certain portion of the profits of the enterprise as stipulated in the corporate charter.[83]

Though there was strong sentiment for the 25 francs share, the Congress did not specifically approve it, instead voting a resolution that the minimum value of shares should be determined by law. A number of resolutions favoring fuller disclosure to be implemented by publishing a special journal, following the Belgian practice, passed. Finally, the Congress would allow stockholders to convoke special stockholders' meetings, and bondholders were to be allowed to attend and speak, but not vote, in stockholders' meetings. This reformed agenda did not receive universal assent. Those who

[81] E. Lecouturier, *Traité des parts de fondateur* (2nd ed.: Paris, 1914), pp. 3-4.
[82] 65AQ G72.
[83] Jurists argued over whether founders' shares constituted a claim on the company or gave their holders equity. Most opinions held for the former and it was this position that the extraparliamentary commission of 1902 adopted.

pushed for increased restrictions were omnipresent, and particularly asser-
tive when financial scandals, bankruptcies and frauds exposed the fallacies
of liberal reform.

The legislature did open the way for the issuing of preferred stock, as
advocated by the International Congress. The utility of preferred stock
(*actions des priorités* or *actions privilégies*), which were so successful in
England, attracted the attention of many authorities, who urged the easing of
their issue in France. Preferred stock confers a prior claim over ordinary
stock to dividends, and, in the event of the dissolution of the company, to
the capital. French law did not prohibit the issue of preferred stock. Such
shares could be issued at the time a company was founded, but it required
the unanimous consent of all shareholders if they were issued subsequently,
which was almost impossible to achieve. For companies in distress it was
impossible to float additional equity shares at par; the issue of bonds could
place a heavy burden on the company by requiring fixed interest payments
that had to be met and the eventual reimbursement of principal. An issue of
preferred shares could avoid these difficulties.

Alexandre Millerand introduced a bill in 1899, which finally became the
law of 9 July 1902 permitting the issue of preferred stock upon approval at a
stockholders' meeting, unless the issue of such stock was specifically forbidden in the company's charter.[84] Unfortunately the new law was so poorly
drafted that doubts immediately arose as to whether or not the provisions of
the new law applied to existing companies, which the legislator intended. To
correct this deficiency, the following year the law of 16 November 1903
explicitly extended the right to issue preferred stock to all existing companies by a simple majority of stockholders. The new law also included
CPAs, which had been omitted from the 1902 law.

Two companies which took advantage of the new law were the Raffinerie
et Sucrerie Say and the Forges et Fonderies d'Alais. The Raffinerie et
Sucrerie Say raised 27.5 MF in 1905, issuing 114,750 shares of par value
200 francs preferred stock at 240 francs. These shares received the right of
preference over regular shares to profits up to 5% of their par value, and
thereafter (less certain deductions for board members and senior managers)
to 35% of remaining profits.[85] The Forges et Fonderies d'Alais issued 3 MF
of preferred stock in 1905 to extricate itself from a difficult financial
position and to pay for necessary capital improvements. These 500 francs
shares carried a 4% cumulative dividend to be distributed before the ordinary shares received anything; they also participated with ordinary shares in

[84] The bill passed both chambers with no debate. *Journal officiel*, Chambre, Débats, séance
du 21 janvier 1902, p. 94 and *Journal officiel*, Sénat, Débats, séance du 19 juin 1902, p. 831.

[85] *Annuaires Desfossés. Annuaire des valeurs admise à la cote officielle de la Bourse de
Paris* (Paris, 1913).

the regular dividend, if any, up to an additional 4%. They were offered to current shareholders first.[86] However, in spite of their popularity and proven utility elsewhere, French companies rarely issued preferred stock.

To deal with other changes in the 1867 and 1893 laws, the government appointed an extraparliamentary commission on 21 June 1902. In spite of sentiment for a complete codification and reform of company law,[87] the commission, the government and parliament opted for piecemeal reform. Although these efforts produced little in the way of actual legislation, the proposals indicated what the problems were and what, if anything, should be done about them. Lack of agreement on many issues contributed to legislative inaction; to legislators, problems of corporate law seldom appeared to be of crucial importance, unless events, like the Rochette affair, thrust them to center stage. The extraparliamentary commission, presided over by Charles Lyon-Caen, with Rodolphe Rousseau as secretary, proposed legislation to cover all pressing matters without resorting to a general codification. Its recommendations were embodied in government bills that were introduced into the Chamber of Deputies on 3 April and 4 July 1903; the following year, on 3 April 1904 they were reported out of committee by Guillaume Chastenet without substantial changes.

The bills aimed at halting abuses in the founding of corporations by requiring fuller disclosure and publicity. Corporate charters were to be published in a special supplement to the *Journal Officiel*; some reformers had sought this reform for almost three decades. The currently popular founders' shares were to be restricted by requiring that, like shares received in exchange for non-pecuniary assets, they be non-negotiable for two years. The bills required that the order form used to subscribe for shares (*bulletin de souscription*) must contain certain basic information on the valuation of physical assets exchanged for shares, and on any special advantages granted to the founders of the company. The proceeds from subscribed shares were to be deposited in one of three designated semi-official banks: The Bank of France, the Caisse de Dépôts et Consignations, or the Crédit Foncier. Unless specified differently in the charter, the principle of one share entitling its holder to one vote in stockholders' meetings was to prevail. The powers of

---

[86] AQ65 K3[1].

[87] As may be assumed, the deficiencies of existing law and the need for codification were most apparent to lawyers. A. Vavasseur criticized piecemeal reform and the "legislative incoherence" of French company law. For example, the law did not cover mergers, which had not been foreseen. *Revue des sociétés*, 21(1903), pp. 86-88. Codification was also supported by a congress on commerce, sponsored by *Le Matin*, and by M. Linol in his brochure *La Codification des lois de capital*, a copy of which was distributed to all members of both chambers. Another jurist, Edmond Thaller, while blaming the 1867 law for financial excesses, believed that only specific remedies were necessary. "Preface" to C. Leouzon le Duc, *La Réforme des sociétés par actions* (Paris, 1910), pp. v-vi.

commissioners elected by stockholders to examine the accounts of a company were to be extended to the whole year, rather than just to verifying the annual reports.

Although the bills failed to make the legislative calendar in the 8th legislature which expired in 1906, they were re-introduced without change in the new legislature on 27 November 1906, and again re-introduced in the 10th legislature on 27 October 1910. Most of these proposals were still pending before the Chamber in 1914, although several proposals did become law. The Finance Law of 30 January 1907, Article 3, required that summaries of corporate charters for companies issuing shares to the public be published in a special supplement of the *Journal Officiel*. In 1912, the name was changed from *Annex au Journal Officiel* to *Bulletin des annonces légales et obligatoire à la charge des sociétés financières*, so it would not appear that the companies were in any way sanctioned by the government. Although this disclosure reform was long sought, the revenues generated by this measure appear to be a major reason for its enactment.[88]

Another proposal of the extraparliamentary committee that became law involved the power of stockholders' meetings to amend corporate charters. Since the law of 1867 gave little guidance, the courts established their own criteria. The courts held that simple changes could be made in the charter by a majority vote at a special stockholders' meeting, while fundamental changes required a unanimous vote of all stockholders. Unfortunately, this jurisprudence was not clear on what constituted **simple** changes and **fundamental** changes. There was general agreement that changing the nationality of the company, or any measure infringing the limited liability of shareholders, was a fundamental change requiring unanimity, which in any company with more than a few stockholders was virtually impossible to achieve. However, jurisprudence was not clear on whether such a matter as changing a company's line of business was a simple or a fundamental change. Contradictory decisions had been rendered on the ability of gas companies to generate and distribute electricity without a unanimous vote of stockholders. Another important area of controversy involved absorption of one company by another, or the merger of two companies.[89] Did these decisions require unanimity? The law of 22 November 1913, which limited amendments to the charter requiring unanimity to changes in the nationality

[88] The charges for publishing these summaries were 4 francs a line, about four times the normal rate.

[89] J. Percerou, "De la nature et de l'étendue des pouvoirs de l'assemblée générale, relativement aux modifications des statuts," Louis Mathieu, ed., *Documents du Congrès Juridique International des Sociétés par Actions et des Sociétés Coopératives* (2 vols., Louvain, 1910), I, pp. 360-61; Gabriel Bourcart, "De la nature et de l'étendue des pouvoirs de l'assemblée générale, relativement aux modifications des statuts," Ibid., I, p. 302ff; E. E. Thaller, *Traité élémentaire de droit commercial* (7th ed., Paris, 1925), pp. 454-63.

of a company and infringement on the limited liability of stockholders, ended conflicting jurisprudence on these matters. However, most of the reform agenda was ignored, even though the Rochette Affair in 1908 gave rise to renewed demands for reform, particularly for the protection of stockholders from unscrupulous promoters.

The Rochette Affair was a classic example of a stock market scandal with overtones of political corruption. Henri Rochette was a company promoter who, starting with little or no capital, managed through lavish publicity to found many companies and issue about 100 MF to 131 MF, according to the official investigator, of overvalued or worthless stock between December 1904 and March 1908.[90] His empire collapsed after his arrest in 1908, allegedly on the orders of no less than the head of the government, Clemenceau, who was said to be acting on behalf of old respectable financial interests interested in destroying the parvenu financier. Nor was Rochette without powerful political friends. The trials of the principals, and two parliamentary investigations chaired by Jean Jaurès, kept the scandal intermittently in the limelight until 1914. The affair revived numerous restrictive proposals for legislation to safeguard savings and protect unwary investors.

The most comprehensive of the restrictive proposals came in 1911 from Maurice Colin, a deputy for Algiers and a professor of the Faculty of Law at the University of Algiers. Colin proposed in his book, *Sur les Mesures à prendre pour défendre l'épargne dans les sociétés par actions*, a complete redrafting of the still pending reform bill on the grounds that investors needed more protection. The allegedly high mortality rate among SAs disturbed Colin. Between 1896 and 1906, approximately 2,800 SAs were dissolved and 4,000 were founded. This signified for Colin, who did not distinguish among the diverse reasons for dissolution, that measures had to be taken to insure greater solidity in SAs. This he proposed to accomplish by adding further restrictions to the bill. He also proposed that legislation be passed tightening the issue of securities. He would forbid the negotiation of shares of a new company for a period of two years, thus applying the same prohibition on all shares that the law of 1893 applied only to stock issued in exchange for non-pecuniary assets. All shares were to be entirely paid-up; non-pecuniary assets were to be appraised by an expert; a professional accountant, appointed by the president of the Commercial Tribunal, should assist the stockholders in verifying the accuracy of financial statements; finally, some uniformity ought to be required of financial statements. For Colin, the restrictions of the German regime for SAs was superior to the

[90] C 7450, Parliamentary Commission on the Rochette Affair. Letter of Rochette to Jaurès, 25 Nov. 1910. The lower estimate is Rochette's. About 2.5 MF were expended on publicity, partly in subsidies to the financial press, partly to fund Rochette's own journal, *La Finance pratique*.

greater freedom found in France. There was little original in these proposals, most of which had been around for a long time.

The presence of so many deputies and senators gracing boards of directors continued to attract criticism, particularly by socialist deputies. Bills that prohibited the assuming of a directorship by a sitting legislator were introduced almost annually. Another proposal would prohibit state contracts from being awarded to any company with a deputy or senator on its board, and forbid any financial institution with legislator-directors from participating in the issue of government bonds.[91]

In spite of the problems, scandals, and crises since 1867, the French corporation emerged basically unchanged from what the law of 1867 had envisioned. Some important changes were made, but the legislator pursued a middle course, deaf to both the call of restrictionists who would minutely regulate the corporation, as in Germany, and the call of liberals who would emulate the less restrictive legislation of the United Kingdom and Belgium, or even go so far as to jettison all regulation. The courts also helped shape the corporation. Charged as they were with the repression of fraud, their jurisprudence tended to be restrictive, but they also exhibited an ability to accommodate legitimate business needs. And finally businessmen, as always, proved to be fertile in expedients to circumvent institutional rigidities.

One of the main purposes of the corporation is to mobilize capital. To the extent that corporations succeed or fail in this endeavor has important implications for economic development. Contemporaries and subsequent scholars criticized financial corporations for hindering domestic economic growth by denying capital to industrial corporations. The next two chapters examine these charges and evaluate the effectiveness of French corporations in providing and securing capital: First, with banks in providing financing for industrial corporations, and second, with industrial corporations in raising adequate capital.

---

[91] Introduced by two radical deputies, Justin Godart and Emile Bender, on 31 January 1911; text in *Revue des sociétés*, 30 (1912), pp. 303-305.

CHAPTER III

LYSIS vs. TESTIS: THE AGE OF FINANCE CAPITAL

. . . on ne peut avoir, en definitive, que le crédit qu'on mérite.

A. Raffalovich, 1912

The Controversy over the Foreign Investment

Although the debate over the effects of capital export on the domestic economy goes back to at least the 1850s, it was Eugène Letailleur, a small businessman turned financial journalist, who transformed it into a minor *cause celèbre* in the years before World War I. There is little that was original in Letailleur's argument, his chief contribution being to present a complete catalog of the charges and to muster a fair amount of supporting evidence. The timing, always crucial in such matters, was favorable as events during 1906 and 1907 helped to focus attention upon Letailleur's charges. France experienced a depression in 1907, and depressions tend to raise critical questions about economic performance. Beginning in 1904, war and subsequent revolution raised fears concerning the value of Russian government bonds, which were widely held in France. The floating of a new loan by the Russian government in the French market in 1906 served as a symbol for the question of foreign lending in general, and helped to thrust it into the political arena.

A similar debate over the pros and cons of capital export took place in Britain, and likewise became a political issue between 1908 and 1914.[1] Conservatives joined leftists in attacking the export of capital, including the ironic spectacle of Viscount Goschen and Lords Rothschild and Revelstoke condemning foreign investment, "no doubt to the astonishment of their

---

[1] Avner Offer, "Empire and Social Reforms: British Overseas Investment and Domestic Politics, 1908-1914," *Historical Journal* XXVI (1983), pp. 119-38.

listeners who were well aware that the families of these three peers had become millionaires precisely by exporting British capital."[2]

In foreign lending the French government played an important role. Before a foreign security could be quoted on the Bourse of Paris, the consent of both the Minister of Foreign Affairs and the Minister of Finance was necessary. This was, in effect, a veto because without the authorization to trade a foreign security on the Bourse, the banks would have difficulty, especially for large issues, in selling foreign stocks and bonds. This led to numerous unofficial contacts between the ministries and bankers before and during loan negotiations. Nor did the ministers always agree.

In 1914 French foreign investments stood at more than 50 billion francs, second in the world only to the United Kingdom and about twice that of Germany. In 1870, French foreign investments amounted to 13.5 billion francs; by 1897 they had almost doubled reaching 26.65 billion francs and over the next 16 years (1898-1913), they almost doubled again reaching 50.4 billion francs.[3] Over this last period, the net annual flow of capital into foreign investment averaged 1.35 billion francs. Encouraged by government policy and a higher rate of return than on French government bonds, by 1914 Russian government bonds constituted more than 20% of the foreign investment total.

Even before the turn of the century, French holdings of Russian government bonds passed 4 billion francs, causing two finance ministers, G. C. P. Cochery in 1897 and 1898, and Joseph Caillaux in 1901, to express reservations about the amount of Russian government borrowing in France.[4] Caillaux opposed the Russian loan of 1901 on financial grounds, but lost to Théophile Delcassé in the cabinet, where the primacy of foreign policy prevailed. Caillaux's objections stemmed from the huge amount of debt already in French hands and the effects of the recession of 1900 on French savings, rather than opposition to foreign lending in general.[5] In addition to political ties, the necessity of creditors to continue lending in order to insure the integrity of past borrowing bound France inextricably to Russia. The outbreak of the Russo-Japanese War in February 1904, which not only caused a rapid plunge in the value of the over 4.75 billion francs (nominal) of Russian government bonds already held in France, but led, under less than advantageous circumstances, to the floating of a war loan of 800 MF in

---

[2] Sidney Pollard, "Capital Exports, 1870-1914: Harmful or Beneficial?" *Economic History Review* 2nd series, XXXVIII (1985), pp. 494-5.
[3] Rondo Cameron, *France and the Economic Development of Europe*, p. 79.
[4] Olga Crisp, *Studies in the Russian Economy Before 1914* (London, 1976), pp. 199 and 204.
[5] Jean Claude Allain, *Joseph Caillaux*, p. 312.

5% five year treasury bonds on the Paris market.[6] The subsequent defeat and revolution forced the Russian government to return once again to the French market for an additional 1.2 billion francs (nominal).

Profits from these operations accruing to French banks were enormous, and earned with little risk. The banks paid 82.5 MF to the Russian treasury for the 5% 1906 bonds, which were offered to the public at 88 MF. Even after the deduction of expenses, including large subsidies to the press for favorable treatment, the members of the loan syndicate enjoyed huge profits, further swelled by various commissions and the free use of large sums until they had to be paid to the Russian treasury.[7] Nor was the French government reluctant to obtain concessions from a needy ally. In 1904, Maurice Rouvier, the head of the government, pressed the Russians to order war materiel from French companies, and in 1906 he linked opening negotiations for the loan with the promise of complete Russian support for the French at the Algeciras conference.[8] With the Russian loan of 1906, the issue of foreign lending, formerly confined to debate by economists, to discussion in the financial press, and to concern in the corridors of the Ministry of Finance, became an issue of broad public interest.

A decade earlier, a meeting of the influential Société d'Economie Politique of Paris discussed the proposition: "Should measures be taken to restrain or prevent investment in foreign securities?"[9] As was to be expected from such a liberal body, opinion was almost uniformly negative. Among the speakers, Raphaël G. Lévy, Arthur Raffalovich, and the Comte de Labry all favored freedom to export capital without the least hindrance. Alfred Neymarck also agreed in principle with the virtually unanimous view that capital export should be unfettered, though he allowed that political considerations might require that one not lend to one's enemies. Another member, Gay, thought that in certain circumstances capital export might be disadvantageous for the domestic economy, but he rejected the view that any measures should be taken to restrain or prevent it. Georges Martin complained that French law governing corporations and tax legislation both "favored investment in foreign securities in preference to investment in French securities."[10] The advantages of foreign investment were not neglected. Foreign lending resulted in orders for French goods and France

6   O. Crisp, *Studies in the Russian Economy*, pp. 199, 200 and 206. These are nominal values. The 1904 loan was issued at 99 MF, taken by the banking syndicate at 95.5 MF, with the Russian treasury, after deduction of expenses, receiving 94 MF.

7   René Girault, *Emprunts Russes et investissements français en Russie, 1887-1914* (Paris, 1973), pp. 444 and 448.

8   Ibid., pp. 403 and 434. The house of Rothschild, in January 1906, refused to aid in a Russian loan unless something was done to improve the lot of Jews in Russia.

9   Meeting of March 5, 1897. *Economiste français*, 13 March 1897, pp. 331-33.

10   Ibid., p. 333.

received an annual return on existing investment of from 1 to 1.2 billion francs.

At the time when Letailleur's *exposé* was just beginning, Paul Leroy-Beaulieu offered to the readers of the *Economiste Français* a detailed explanation for the huge capital outflow.[11] The French, he believed, saved more than other nations, while at the same time there was a relatively lower domestic demand for capital. The low domestic demand stemmed from France's stable population, her relatively stable domestic market, and her low level, and costly, production of coal. Much recent industrial development (he cited automobiles and phonographs) absorbed only small amounts of capital. The expansion of hydroelectric power may require larger amounts, but this development was barely underway. The surpluses actually began with the stagnation of investment in railroads. "What is needed is a great invention, requiring enormous productive installations, to come to the rescue and provide a new impulsion."[12] But Leroy-Beaulieu placed greater emphasis on social fears than on purely economic reasons:[13]

> The most effective cause for the exodus of French capital is the fear of capitalists and rentiers. The specters that the government, the parliament, and the candidates have evoked with regard to "acquired wealth" spread terror among these groups (*couches sociales*), who are easily alarmed. They send their capital over the border, and, if the menace is pushed much further, some of them may cross the border themselves.

He advised Parliament to reflect on the Revocation of the Edict of Nantes.

It was the views of these liberal economists that Letailleur challenged when he published a series of sensational articles under the pen name of Lysis in *La Revue* in 1906 and 1907, which were printed as a book in 1908 with the same inflammatory title, *Contre l'oligarchie financière en France*. The 1908 printing of the book was said to be 35,000 copies,[14] a huge figure for this sort of book. With the original text slightly revised, but greatly lengthened with the inclusion of a long response to his chief critic, Letailleur's tract reached 11 printings by 1916.[15] Though not a socialist, Lysis later wrote a series of articles for Jaurès' *L'Humanité* in which he attempted to show how the export of capital injured the interests of the working man. Lysis, who was an ardent nationalist, found even more damning the lack of patriotism of French bankers, which he later exposed in *Les Capitalistes français contre la France* (1916).

[11] "L'Exode des capitaux français," *Economiste français*, 28 May 1906, pp. 729-31.
[12] Ibid., p. 730.
[13] Ibid., p. 731.
[14] Edouard Blanc, "La vie de Lysis," in *Pages Inachevées* (Paris, 1928), p. 7.
[15] His reply to Testis appeared first in the *Grande Revue*.

Lysis made two basic charges: (1) A few huge banks, through their control over the mobilization and employment of French savings, constituted an omnipotent financial oligarchy. (2) These savings were directed primarily into the bonds of foreign governments to the detriment of domestic industry, particularly small provincial enterprises, which found it impossible to obtain credit.

These big banks had extinguished competition. They either divided up the market and respected each others' territory, or for large operations, formed syndicates in which they shared, especially for the foreign loan business. The formerly important private bankers of Paris known as the *haute banque*, and provincial banks, which were declining in numbers and importance from the competition with branches of the big banks, found themselves relegated to a minor role. The financial oligarchy consisted of the three leading deposit banks: The Crédit Lyonnais (1863), the Société Générale (1864), and the Comptoir National d'Escompte (1889, successor to the Comptoir d'Escompte, which failed the same year). Also included in the oligarchy was the Banque de Paris et des Pays Bas (Paribas), formed in 1872 by the merger of the Banque de Paris (1870) and a Dutch bank, Paribas, an investment bank, which did not accept deposits from the public. All were joint-stock banks, and the three deposit banks maintained many branch offices in Paris and the provinces. Of 244 branch offices for the Crédit Lyonnais in 1908, 173 were in the provinces, 53 in Paris, and 18 abroad. In the same year, the Société Générale had 89 branch offices in Paris and 638 in the provinces. The deposits of the three deposit banks in 1908 amounted to 562.7 MF for the Société Générale, 632.1 for the Comptoir National d'Escompte, and 798.3 MF for the Crédit Lyonnais, totaling almost 2 billion francs. By comparison, the deposits for the Crédit Industriel et Commercial (CIC), which was not a small bank, were 94.5 MF.[16]

Although Lysis regarded these four banks as dominant, he identified a second, and less important group that included two old banks, the CIC (1859) and the Société Marseillaise (1865) and two recently created banks, the Banque de l'Union Parisienne (1904) and the Banque Française pour le Commerce et l'Industrie (1901), presided over by Maurice Rouvier.

The preference of the large banks for large operations made it difficult for small borrowers. Lysis alleged that the oligarchy was hostile to French industry, citing a statement that Henri Germain made at the annual shareholders' meeting of the Crédit Lyonnais in 1903 in which Germain justified the bank's lack of investment in French industry. The views of the late Henri Germain, according to Lysis, continued to dominate the views of the big banks. As a result, the amounts of foreign bond issues dwarfed the small

---

[16] The figures on deposits and the number of branches are drawn from: Alfred Neymarck, *Les Etablissements de crédit en France depuis cinquante ans* (Paris, 1909), a paper read to the Statistical Society of Paris on 17 February 1909.

number and amount of domestic industrial issues underwritten by the oligarchy. The banks were unpatriotic for neglecting domestic industry, and for extending loans even to France's enemies. The foreign issues ended in the coffers of French *rentiers*, who were "sheep led by bad shepherds."

According to Lysis, financial concentration was not an irreversible trend of the times. Neither the United Kingdom nor the United States possessed a comparable degree of concentration. The degree of concentration in France exceeded even that of Germany where, unlike France, banks invested heavily in domestic industry. This concentration permitted the banks to control the Bourse, whose 70 brokers were dependent upon them and obediently listed all securities that the big banks patronized. The press was also in the thrall of the oligarchy being financially dependent and hence subservient. Finally, the banks reaped exorbitant profits and gave poor service, especially to those involved in promoting French exports, who often received better terms from foreign banks.

Lysis proposed that the state intervene to bring an end to this intolerable state of affairs. There should be a strict separation of investment and deposit banking. Banks that received deposits from the public should be prohibited from underwriting, as was the case in the United Kingdom. Further, the government must be given the right to intervene in determining the use of French savings. The stamp tax on foreign government bonds should be raised from 1 to 2% (a proposal Minister of Finance Caillaux incorporated into the budget for 1907). Finally, the government should encourage the creation of provincial banks to promote regional development.

The establishment's response to Lysis' damning indictment appeared in 1907, as a series of articles in the *Revue politique et parlementaire*. It was later collected and published separately under the title *Le Rôle des établissements de crédit en France; La verité sur les propos de Lysis* (1907), under the pen name of Testis, a pseudonym for Raphaël G. Lévy, a prominent banker and contributor of articles on financial subjects to influential periodicals. Testis rejected the view that the big banks did not compete among themselves, as well as the view that the *haute banque* and local banks had been relegated to a minor role. He pointed out that the Rothschilds led in the negotiation of Russian government loans between 1889 and 1901, and only abstained thereafter to express disapproval over the treatment of Jews in Russia. The separation between the *haute banque* and the joint-stock banks Testis regarded as artificial: members of the *haute banque* often had interest in, or controlled, the giant banks. He also cited examples where the big banks competed for foreign loans, and subsequently floated them alone rather than forming a syndicate, though he recognized that for large operations syndicates, including representatives of the *haute banque*, were used. In short, the dominance of the big banks was far from complete, and they did compete.

Were the big banks hostile to French industry and was the export of capital detrimental to France? In his answer, Testis made a distinction between long and short-term credit. Far from having denied short-term credit to commerce and industry, the large institutions extended it more freely and at a lower rate than formerly. He recognized that many local banks disappeared as a result of the competitive struggle with branches of the big Paris-based banks. But he argued big banks helped provide capital for large industrial enterprises by underwriting industrial issues of stocks and bonds, and smaller banks performed the same function for smaller enterprises. Although Testis denied that the banks were hostile to French industry, he admitted that they only partially satisfied industrial needs for long-term credit, particularly to small enterprises. Extending long-term credit, or the taking of a direct interest in industrial enterprises, large or small, was too risky, and as Henri Germain had emphasized on numerous occasions, it was not within the legitimate or wise operations of a deposit bank. Testis concluded: "The right of every French citizen to credit is not written yet . . . in our constitution."[17] Banks were private enterprises. "They are not charged with carrying on a public service and they do not enjoy the irresponsibility that representatives of the State enjoy."[18] They were responsible to the owners of 1.6 million shares.

Citing Leroy-Beaulieu, Testis blamed low population growth and the lack of cheap coal for the relatively low level of demand for industrial capital. The possibility of entrepreneurial failure was not mentioned, but strikes and labor indiscipline were. Under these circumstances, the banks by facilitating the export of excess capital performed a beneficial and patriotic service to the nation. Not only did foreign loans provide income, they also increased French exports. While Testis cited examples of orders to French industry financed by loans to Russia,[19] Lysis countered with examples where the proceeds of French loans were spent in England, or worst of all, Germany.

Others joined in the controversy. Alfred Neymarck defended the big banks in an address to the Statistical Society of Paris in February 1909, his remarks subsequently appearing in the columns of *Le Rentier*, which he edited. Neymarck particularly defended the refusal of banks to make long-term loans to industrial and commercial enterprises as wise. He quoted approvingly Henri Germain's statement to the stockholders' meeting of the Crédit Lyonnais of 1902: "[Lending to] even the best conceived and wisely administered industrial enterprises involves risks that we consider as incom-

---

[17] Testis, *Le Rôle des établissements de crédit* (Paris, 1907), p. 77.
[18] Ibid., p. 78.
[19] Arthur Raffalovich furnished Testis with the information. R. Girault, "Portrait de l'homme d'affaires Français vers 1914," *Revue d'histoire moderne et contemporaine*, XVI (1969), pp. 331-2.

patible with the indispensable security in the use of a deposit bank's funds."[20]

Jules Domergue, the editor of *Réforme Economique*, an organ sponsored by protectionists, came to the defense of Lysis. Neymarck, he stated, "has only praise for those 'financial instruments' which appear to him to have attained the ultimate degree of perfection."[21] Although Neymarck found eleven reasons to praise the banks, he offered not a single criticism, an omission Domergue hastened to correct. Lysis' main points were still intact, though Domergue admitted that Testis had corrected some exaggerations. Domergue reiterated Lysis' arguments, adducing additional evidence to support them, and added a few charges of his own concerning the lack of support by the banks for France's export effort. Domergue also lamented the lack of any contribution by the banks toward promoting economic development in the French colonies. He noted that the Comptoir National d'Escompte had 6 or 7 offices in Madagascar, but what has it done to promote the development of the island? "The answer is easy. The Comptoir d'Escompte has done nothing."[22]

The views of Lysis and Testis and their respective supporters would seem to reflect the existence of an intra-class struggle between the financial and industrial capitalists. But the internal cohesiveness of these two groups is open to question. The industrialists were not united as many fared well in the new era. Even the symbol of the bankers, the late master of the Crédit Lyonnais, Henri Germain, had not always been a defender of the export of capital. Speaking in the National Assembly in 1875, Germain defended the construction of local railroads, partly on the grounds that they would provide needed investment opportunities for French capital. In the absence of these opportunities, he continued, "French capital, to the detriment of the nation's wealth, crosses the frontier and finds investments in foreign lands."[23] Circumstances change as do men. The issue was not confined to differing groups of capitalists as the attack on the big banks united many

[20] A. Neymarck, *Les Etablissements de crédit en France cinquante ans*, p. 42. See also the anonymous "La Querelle de Lysis et de Testis jugée par Minos," *Journal des économistes*, XXVII (1908), pp. 93-101.

[21] Jules Domergue, *La Question des sociétés de crédit* (Bar le Duc, 1909), p. 66. First published in *La Réforme économique*.

[22] Ibid., p. 38. An anonymous pamphlet by "X," *L'Exportation française et les établissements de crédit* (1909) argued that the banks adequately financed French exports, and attack a proposal, emanating from the French embassy in London, to create a large export bank. Other responses to Domergue came from Yves Guyot, "La Campagne contre les sociétés de crédit," *Journal des économistes*, XXIV (Nov. 1909), pp. 172-88, and Alfred Neymarck in an address to the Société d'Economie Politique in October 1909 on the large banks and the concentration of capital, *Journal des économistes*, XXIV (Oct. 1909), pp. 84-100.

[23] Séance du 25 mai 1875. In *Discours parlementaires de Henri Germain sur les finances*, 2 vols. (Paris, 1885), I, 325. I am indebted to Sanford Elwitt for this reference.

diverse interests: small and medium-size commerce and industry, local bankers and notaries, laborers, nationalists, and the Left in the Chamber could identify with, and make use of, the alleged culpability of the big banks. The whole debate raised important questions, and if the participants in this heated controversy were less than objective, the merits of the charges bear further scrutiny. In the following pages will be examined, first, the place of the large Parisian banks in the banking system, and second, the relationship between banks and industry.

The Structure of the Banking System

Did the big banks control the economy? Allegations about the dominance of high finance were not confined to France. Rudolf Hilferding expressed similar views for Germany in *Finance Capital* (1910),[24] views which Lenin later incorporated into his theory of imperialism.[25] In Germany, however, the Hilferding-Lenin formulation differed from the French variant: the *Grossbankens* dominated the economy through their strong support of domestic industry, a domination all the more effective because of increasing cartelization. Concentration was less in England because deposit banks could not engage in underwriting, though J. A. Hobson charged that financial interests were the directing force in British imperial expansion after 1870. In the United States, populists and progressives, farmers and muckrakers voiced complaints about the power of bankers, focusing upon J. P. Morgan, though banking laws in the United States limited the degree of financial concentration. In France, it seemed that the power of banks was growing along with their increasing size and concentration, a development which the corporate form of business organization facilitated. Though there was little change in function between the traditional private banks and the new joint-stock banks, the latter outdistanced their sometime rivals in the size of their resources. The creation of branches in the provinces greatly increased their resources and destroyed many local banks in the process.

At the beginning of the 19th century every town and village had one or more persons who functioned as a banker, be it part-time, combined with the functions of a notary or a merchant (such as M. l'Heureux, the merchant of Yonville who lent money to Emma Bovary) or full-time, particularly in

[24] The first French translation of this important work appeared only in 1970, and the first English translation not until 1981.

[25] The Hobson-Lenin thesis that capital export was the main motive of the "new" imperialism ill fits France, but the contention that an oligarchy of banks controlled the economy deserves serious consideration. Lenin, of course, saw imperialism as an inevitable stage in capitalist development, while for Hobson, imperialism was only a bad policy that could be reformed by a more equitable distribution of income at home.

larger towns. These bankers, benefiting from their quasi-monopoly position, charged high rates of interest. But even before mid-century and before the coming of any of the large deposit banks, the local monopolies were beginning to break down because of growing competition, in part owing to the creation of branches of the Bank of France and joint-stock departmental banks. By 1848, 13 branches of the Bank of France, created between 1836 and 1848, joined the nine joint-stock departmental banks, created between 1817 and 1838, to serve the larger commercial and industrial centers, and help bring down interest rates. During the crisis of 1848, the departmental banks lost their autonomy and became branches of the Bank of France. The creation of *caisses d'épargnes* (savings banks) to inculcate the virtue of thrift within the working class, but which had an equal appeal to the middle class, channeled local savings into government bonds and deprived local lenders of a source of capital. The 27 *caisses d'épargnes* of 1833 grew to 354 with 175 branch offices by the end of 1847.[26] Even more important, the establishment of a *grand livre auxiliaire* in each department in 1819 to facilitate the buying and selling of government bonds, followed by a decrease in the minimum size of the *rente* in 1822, opened the way to a greatly expanded holding of *rentes* in the provinces.[27] The Bank of France continued its expansion after mid-century. In 1855, the Bank conducted business at 205 locations; legislation in 1897 required the bank to maintain a branch office in every departmental seat.[28]

The spread of branches of the Bank of France to the provinces only partly posed a competitive threat to the existence of local banks. To a large extent they complemented one another. The local banks acted as the necessary intermediaries between borrowers and the local branch of the Bank of France. The network of local banks probably reached its apogee in the 1860s.[29] As the research of Alain Plessis has revealed, at the end of the Second Empire there existed "an unsuspectedly rich banking network" of about 3,000 banks, 2,500 of which were outside the Paris area.[30] The number of provincial banks fell thereafter, partly as a result of the coming of the branches of large banks, but competition among local banks, and mergers, also played an important role. The laments over the demise of small local banks pictured the local banker as a person who lived in the community, knew its problems intimately, and served its needs adequately. Critics

---

[26] C. Freedeman, "French Securities Market," p. 78.

[27] Ibid., pp. 76-77.

[28] Gabriel Ramon, *Banque de France*, pp. 403 and 424.

[29] Alain Plessis, "Le 'retard francais:' la faute à la banque? Banques locales, succurales de la Banque de France et financement de l'économie sous le Second Empire" in *Le Capitalisme français, XIXe-XXe siècle; blocages et dynamismes d'une croissance* edited by Patrick Fridenson and André Straus (Paris, 1987), p. 204.

[30] Ibid.

contrasted this idealized picture to the impersonal and routine operations of branches of the large credit institutions, where important decisions were made by faceless men in Paris who lacked knowledge of, and interest, in local conditions.

But provincial banks persisted, both joint-stock and private, prospering in spite of competition from Paris. The survival, regrouping, and adaptation of provincial banks in the face of outside competition is worth looking at in greater detail. Although a great deal of research remains to be done on this subject, it is possible to see the general trends.

The most obvious development to the critics of the large Parisian banks was the decline in the number of provincial banks, from about 2,500 at the beginning of the Third Republic to less than 1,000. They ignored the strength and vitality of the survivors, many of which were joint-stock banks. These developments may be seen in Nancy, which became the financial center of the East (Department of Meurthe et Moselle) after the disappearance of Mulhouse, Strasbourg, and Metz into the German Empire in 1871. Here, five medium to large-sized banks, with a regional orientation, organized either as SAs or CPAs, emerged from a milieu of small private local banks.[31] The two largest were the Société Nancéienne de Crédit Industriel et Commercial and the Banque Renauld et Cie.. The first was founded as an SA on the basis of a small discount house in 1881 with a nominal capital of 16 MF (4 MF paid-in). The capital of the Société Nancéienne was raised in 1899, 1905, 1907 and 1910[?], reaching 60 MF (one-quarter called). The Banque Renauld was founded in 1878 on the basis of a small private bank with capital of 1 MF; it became a CPA in 1889 capitalized at 2 MF, which with further increases attained 20 MF by 1910. During the same period branch offices of the Société Générale (1872), the Crédit Lyonnais (1881), and the Comptoir National d'Escompte (1899) opened in Nancy. The Bank of France established a branch office in Nancy in 1853.

Here, as elsewhere, the competition of the branch banks, limited as it was to short term credit, helped to re-orient the functions of regional banks to types of business where they possessed advantages over Parisian banks, encouraging them to enter into areas in which the branch banks dared not enter. Many local borrowers discovered that they had to wait for their loans to be approved in Paris, or that at the slightest economic downturn, the conditions of borrowing became suddenly more stringent, or worse, that credit could be completely cut off. The branch banks did little to satisfy medium or long-term credit needs. In this risky area, regional and local banks had the field to themselves. In some rapidly developing areas, such as

---

[31] Claude Collot, "Nancy, métropole financière de la Lorraine, 1871-1914," *Annales de l'Est* 25 (1973), pp. 3-75 and Philippe Jacquemard, *Les Banques Lorraines* (Paris, 1911).

the East, the appearance of a well developed regional banking network closely integrated with local industries took shape.

The banks of Nancy patronized the expansion of the metallurgical, textile, and chemical industries of the region: underwriting the issue of regional securities averaged 12 MF annually for the period 1899-1905 and 46 MF annually for the period 1906-1912.[32] In the absence of a local stock exchange, the banks acted as intermediaries in the buying and selling of regional securities. In Nancy, and elsewhere, regional banks placed the issues they patronized directly with their clients. Since the Bourse was not used as an intermediary in these transactions, they escaped the new issues tax, while at the same time they also escaped public attention. As Arthur Raffalovich pointed out in 1910, the new issues tax does not reflect regional financing of industry.[33] The growth of these banks in Nancy must be viewed in large part as a response to local needs, but in turn the power of the banks gave them a certain amount of control over the development and orientation of regional industry.[34] Industrialists participated in the founding of many regional banks and sat on their boards.

At a meeting of the Société Centrale des Banques de Province, a trade organization with a membership of about 400 provincial banks, held in Nancy in 1909, Charles Renauld (of the Banque Renauld et Cie. of Nancy) discussed some of the advantages of regional banks over the branches of the Paris banks. The decisions of the provincial banks could not be reviewed and reversed by a distant superior in Paris. Provincial banks were more flexible because of their expert knowledge of local conditions, and they provided expert advice and continuing guidance as well as financing. Local borrowers knew that these services were worth a little more.[35]

The North (Nord and Pas de Calais Departments) also possessed a strong and prosperous network of regional banks.[36] The largest, the Crédit du Nord, resembled the large rival Paris banks. Originating in the Comptoir d'Escompte de Lille, founded in 1848, it was transformed into the Société de Crédit Industriel et de Dépôts du Nord in 1866, an SA capitalized at 20 MF. In 1871 it shortened its name to the Crédit du Nord. At the end of the century it underwent a period of rapid expansion, raising its nominal capital from 20 to 30 MF in 1900, to 60 MF in 1910, and to 120 MF in 1914, the last for the acquisition of another important regional bank, the Banque

---

[32] C. Collot, "Nancy, métropole financière," pp. 55 and 72.

[33] A. Raffalovich, *Le Marché Financier, Année économique et financier, 1908-1909*, pp. 382-83.

[34] C. Collot, "Nancy, métropole financière," p. 75.

[35] A. Raffalovich, *Le Marché Financier, 1909-1910*, pp. 320-24.

[36] Jacques Laloux, *Le Rôle des banques locales et régionales du Nord de la France dans le développement industriel et commercial* (Paris, 1924), p. 136; A. Raffalovich, *Le Marché Financier, 1911-1912*, p. 328.

Henri Devilder et Cie.. The Crédit du Nord expanded throughout the region, establishing its first branch at nearby Roubaix in the 1870s; by 1900 the bank possessed 12 branches (*succursales*) or offices (*comptoirs*), including one in Paris, the total growing to 44 by 1914.[37] The largest of the regional banks, controlled from the beginning by merchants and industrialists of the region, the Crédit du Nord concentrated on deposit and short-term credit functions.

In addition to the Crédit du Nord, the region was served by several other large regional banks:[38] (1) The Banque Générale du Nord et du Pas de Calais, founded in 1888 and capitalized at 20 MF. It was the successor to the Caisse Commerciale de Lille, Verley Decroix et Cie., a CPA founded in 1858, capitalized initially at 3 MF. By 1914, it possessed 21 branch offices. (2) The Banque L. Dupont et Cie. at Valenciennes, founded in 1819, it became a CPA in 1846, capitalized initially at 5 MF, rising to 20 MF by 1910. It had 8 branch offices, some of which were successors to local banks. (3) The Banque Adam at Boulogne sur Mer, which existed before the Revolution. A partnership during the 19th century, it became an SA in 1911. Capitalized at 25 MF, it had 29 branch offices by 1914. (4) The Banque Scalbert, the oldest bank in Lille, a large private bank which became an SA in 1920, capitalized at 30 MF. There were more than half a dozen medium-size banks, capitalized at several million francs or more. Some were private banks; others were joint-stock companies, but there was a tendency for private banks to transform themselves into CPAs or SAs.

There were fewer banks in the region in 1914 than in 1870, but counting branch offices, it is unlikely that the region possessed fewer banking offices (even excluding the branches of Paris banks), or fewer banking resources. Both the East (Meurthe et Moselle) and the North (Nord and Pas de Calais) possessed strong banking structures, but with significant differences. One difference was the importance of underwriting in the East and its virtual absence in the North. Unlike the East, which had no local Bourse, the North possessed an active local Bourse at Lille. What the two regions had in common was that both were regions of rapid economic expansion. The services provided by local and regional banks were largely shaped by the demands of local commerce and industry. The banking structure of other regions about which we have some information, was largely shaped by local needs, and exhibits both similarities and differences from that of the East and North. It may be surmised that in relatively stagnant agricultural regions, the creation of branches of the Paris banks deprived local banks of their chief functions without leaving much in the way of alternatives. But, in general, the evidence points to an increase in the number of medium-size

---

[37] 65AQ A753, annual reports of the Crédit du Nord.
[38] J. Laloux, *La Rôle des banques du Nord*, p. 53ff.

banks, both regional and Parisian, in the years before the war. In its annual report for 1912, the Crédit Lyonnais noted that in 1901 there were 57 banks in France and Algeria with a paid-in capital of under 50 MF which published a financial statement at least once a year. In 1911, the number had increased to 103, and the total capital of these banks had increased from 428 MF to 975 MF, and branch offices from 175 to 617.[39] The survival and adaptation of local and regional banks is at variance with the charges leveled by critics of the large Paris banks.

The foregoing examination of the development of the banking structure is not intended to minimize the importance of the large Parisian banks, but to place them within the context of the whole structure. As the critics correctly noted, the invasion of the provinces by branches of the large Parisian banks effected significant changes both locally and nationally. In 1870, the Société Générale, the Crédit Lyonnais, and the Comptoir d'Escompte possessed a total of 47 branch offices outside the Paris area; by 1912 the number had reached 1,303. Table 3.1 shows the expansion of these three banks both in the provinces and in Paris.

Table 3.1 Growth of Parisian and Provincial Branches of the Société Générale, the Crédit Lyonnais, and the Comptoir d'Escompte

	Prov. Branches	*Paris Branches*	*Total*
Société Générale			
1870	42	15	57
1880	101	38	139
1890	116	39	155
1900	287	57	344
1912	903	98	1001
Crédit Lyonnais			
1870	2	1	3
1880	23	29	52
1890	73	23	96
1900	136	34	170
1912	231	59	290

[39] Cited in a report of the Senate's Finance Committee, *Journal officiel*, Sénat, Documents parlementaires, 1915, Annexe No. 195, p. 84.

	Prov. Branches	Paris Branches	Total
Comptoir National d'Escompte			
1870	3	1	4
1880	3	1	4
1890	3	4	7
1900	82	29	110
1912	169	59	228

Source: E. Kaufmann, *La Banque en France* (Paris, 1914), p. 483.

These three so-called deposit banks, plus the Crédit Industriel et Commercial (CIC), whose size and operations was distinctly inferior to the big three, go back to the Second Empire. Of the Parisian investment banks, Paribas was one of the few survivors of the wave of banks founded during the period 1871-1881, while the Banque Française pour le Commerce et l'Industrie and the Banque de l'Union Parisienne were part of a new wave of foundings which began after the turn of the century. The following table shows the growth of these banks during the Third Republic:

Table 3.2 Growth in Capitalization of Large Parisian Banks

	Capital Change	Nominal capital (MF)
Comptoir d'Escompte	reorganized 1854	20
(founded 1848)	1860	40
	1866	80
	reorganized 1889	40 (½ called)
	1889	80 (½ called)
	1892	75
	1895	100
	1900	150
	1909	200
Crédit Lyonnais	1863	20 (½ called)
(founded 1863)	1872	50 (½ called)
	1879	100
	1891	200
	1900	250
Société Générale	1864	120 (¼ called)
(founded 1864)	1866	120 (½ called)
	1899	160 (½ called)
	1903	200 (½ called)
	1905	250 (½ called)
	1906	300 (½ called)
	1909	400 (½ called)
	1912	500 (½ called)

	Capital Change	Nominal capital (MF)
Crédit Industriel et	1859	60 (¼ called)
Commercial	1900	80 (¼ called)
	1906	100 (¼ called)
Banque de Paris et	1872	125 (½ called)
de Pays-Bas	1878	62.5
	1907	75
	1912	100
Banque Française pour le Commerce et l'Industrie	1901	60
Banque de l'Union Parisienne	1904	40
	1905	60
	1913	80

The increases in capital were normally larger than the nominal figures as the new issues often sold at hefty premiums. For example, in 1909, the Société Générale issued 200,000 new shares (par value 500 francs, 250 francs called) at 650 francs and in 1912 an additional 200,000 shares at 785 francs. In 1912 Paribas issued 50,000 new shares (par value 500 francs) at 1,450 and the Comptoir National d'Escompte in 1909 added 100,000 new shares (par value 500 francs) at 650.

According to the critics, the Crédit Lyonnais, Paribas, the Société Générale, and the Comptoir National d'Escompte constituted a controlling, non-competing oligarchy, with which the remainder of the banking structure collaborated as the price for survival. It is true that after 1905 there were close ties between Paribas and the Société Générale.[40] Although the size of the big four and the volume of their deposits was enormous, amounting to half or more the national totals, it is questionable if they controlled the remainder of the banking structure. Even in Paris, the smaller joint-stock banks, as well as the *haute banque*, continued to play an important, and often independent, role. A number of *haute banque* firms, allied with the Belgian Société Générale, founded the Banque de l'Union Parisienne as a rival to Paribas.[41] The relationship of the *haute banque* and the big four was neither always antagonistic nor subservient. Like members of the big four themselves, they competed with each other and with the larger banks, and they collaborated as circumstances dictated.

Although some of the critics claimed that the short-term needs of commerce and industry were not always adequately met, the main question

[40] Edmond Baldy, *Les Banques d'affaires en France depuis 1900* (Paris, 1922), p. 89.

[41] 65AQ A257[1]. The BUP was the successor of the Banque Parisienne founded in 1874. Most of its activities were foreign, particularly the foreign loan business and interests in Russia, Latin America and the Balkans; domestically, it was interested in electric companies.

involved the availability of medium and long-term credit. The tradition of financing expansion through the plough back of profits remained strong among French industrialists even after other sources of finance became available. In any case, there is abundant evidence to suggest that large enterprises, and new sectors (electricity, autos, chemicals, electrometallurgy and urban transport) did not suffer for lack of financing. The large deposit banks and Paribas sponsored many issues of stocks and bonds, and the metallurgical industry of the East was similarly financed by the regional banks of Nancy. A specialty of the provincial banks were *avances sur comptes courants*, extending medium-term credit, as in the North (Nord and Pas de Calais). The role of the Banque Charpenay of Grenoble, and of dozens of other regional banks suggests that French industrial enterprises were adequately provided with medium and long-term financing. The Banque Charpenay, which was founded in 1860 by a wholesale cloth dealer, illustrates the impact of a bank on a region.[42] The bank remained a partnership until 1920 with its capital gradually increasing from 300,000 francs to 2.5 MF in 1913. It patronized primarily the hydro-electric industry of the region (including generation, distribution, traction, electro-metallurgy and electrochemical) and the paper industry. Between 1888 and 1930 it acted as the intermediary in the issue of 43 MF of stock and 131 MF of bonds for 36 firms, as well as provided them with long and short-term financing.[43] The bank's re-discounts with the Bank of France totaled 58 MF in 1913.[44]

This is not an isolated example. The central organ for regional banks, the Syndicat des Banques de Province, noted in its annual report for 1911 that its members had placed over the previous five years more than 500 MF of regional and local issues.[45] The entry of the Syndicat des Banques de Province into the foreign issues business suggests it had more funds at its disposal than it could employ elsewhere.

The complaints that French industry was starved for capital originated in large part from marginal industrialists, who through incompetence, technological obsolescence, or lack of competitive advantages were poor risks. The complaints came from publicists, unhappy with the pace of French economic growth and seeking to assess blame; they came from nationalists, both superpatriots and high tariff men who were disturbed by the huge foreign investment portfolio; finally, they came from the left, providing a convenient stick to beat monopoly finance capitalism.[46]

---

[42] Georges Charpenay, *Les Banques régionalistes* (Paris, 1939).
[43] Ibid., p. 33.
[44] Ibid., p. 32.
[45] E. Baldy, *Les Banques d'affaires*, p. 207.
[46] And they still do. See Henri Claude, *Histoire, Réalité et destin d'un monopole, La Banque de Paris et des Pays-Bas et son groupe* (Paris, 1969), pp. 31-32.

The Banks and Domestic Industry

Did the flow of funds abroad, in which the large Paris banks acted as intermediaries, deprive domestic industry of much needed capital? Not only was this a common charge at the time, but this view has found support among later scholars.[47]

Capital export must be viewed in context with France's international economic position. First, France enjoyed a favorable balance of payments on current account, despite a deficit on the commodity trade balance after 1867 and despite the import of bullion,[48] both of which reduced the sums available for foreign investment. According to the calculations of Rondo Cameron, the average annual net favorable balance on current account amounted to 550 MF during the Second Empire, climbed to 700 MF for the period 1871-1881, fell to 500 MF (1882-1897) and reached 1,350 MF for the period 1898-1913.[49] For countries with a favorable balance of trade, the export of capital is a logical course. Second, the flow of capital export coincided positively with trends in the domestic economy, rising during periods of economic expansion and falling during periods of depression and stagnation. Finally, the sums invested abroad did not constitute an ongoing drain on French savings, because the income on foreign investment throughout the period was more than sufficient to cover new investment. Therefore, the implicit assumption by critics of foreign investment that it constituted an ongoing drain, reducing the amount of capital available for domestic investment, is false. Surprisingly, few of the contemporaries who defended foreign investment made effective use of this argument.[50]

Thus France, given her economic position, like the oil rich countries of the 1970s and Japan in the 1980s, was constrained, barring a rise in domestic imports, to maintain a given level of foreign investment. This investment was not without its advantages for domestic industry, as it often provided both orders for French manufacturers and access to raw materials for French industry. Other inducements to foreign investment mentioned prominently by contemporaries, and which undoubtedly played a small role, included giving the investing public what they wanted, particularly fixed

[47] For example, Harry D. White, *The French International Accounts, 1880-1913* (Cambridge, Mass., 1933), p. 297 and Robert Goffin, *Les Valeurs mobilières en France à la Fin du XIXe siècle (1873-1913)* (Paris, 1967), pp. 140-46.

[48] Rondo Cameron, *France and the Economic Development of Europe*, pp. 79-80.

[49] Ibid., p. 79.

[50] Two exceptions were Henry Lowenfeld, an English economist writing in a French journal, who recognized that current capital export was a product of past investment which, he argued, could only be reduced by an increase in merchandise imports, and Charles Chaumet, a deputy, who estimated that in 1913 the annual income from previous investment exceeded new investment by about 100 MF annually. *France-Univers*, 15 août 1913, pp. 3 and 17.

revenue securities of foreign states, which provided a higher rate of return of between 1 and 2% over comparable French securities, and more favorable tax treatment.[51] Although banks were not without influence over foreign investment, particularly in regard to the choice of type and place of the investment, their role may more accurately be viewed **generally** as that of an intermediary responding to existing economic conditions.

This still leaves the question of the relationship between banks and French industrial firms. When examined from the demand side, the problem is complex. Were French industrialists unable to satisfy their needs for capital and credit? The needs of firms varied according to their size, location, sector and many other variables. Anyone who concentrated only on marginal or troubled enterprises could argue that industry was starved for credit. In fact, seldom would a large, well-managed corporation with a record for profitable operation, experience any difficulty in raising additional equity capital through the sale of stock, or borrowing by the issue of bonds, or securing normal short term credit, except in times of financial crisis. Banks always stood ready to assist such enterprises. As Claude Fohlen pointed out, technical innovations, even when costly, were rapidly adopted, which is a good test for the availability of financing. He cited the adoption of the Bessemer process, the growth of aluminum and electro-chemical enterprises as examples.[52] A cursory examination of the boards of directors of banks and of large industrial enterprises reveals links that ought to dispel the myth of the alleged opposition of bankers and industrialists.

The financial practices of corporations, which will be treated more fully in the next chapter, greatly reduced the demand for external financing. For many, reinvestment of profits was the order of the day. It was considered prudent managerial practice to build up large reserves, and finance expansion from retained earnings.[53] But there was flexibility, and businessmen based their decisions on what circumstances seemed to require. The metallurgical firm of Allevard, which Pierre Léon has analyzed, affords one example of the relationship between a medium-size firm and banks. From

---

[51] Minister of Finance Joseph Caillaux argued in 1907 that the tax advantages of foreign bonds over domestic industrial issues helped channel savings into foreign investments. Domestic stocks paid a 4% tax on dividends and a 1% transfer tax, which foreign government bonds escaped. Caillaux's proposal to end these advantages brought an immediate reaction from the banks. This proposal was not enacted, but the new issues tax was raised from 1 to 2%. (Finance Law of 30 January 1907). The raising of the new issues tax placed French banks at a disadvantage in the foreign loan market since other lenders had either lower rates (Britain 1/2 of 1%; Germany 5/8 of 1%), or no tax at all. The Finance Law of 31 July 1913 raised the new issue tax to 3%, and the following year a 4% tax was levied on the interest payments of foreign government bonds. Joseph Caillaux, *Mes Mémoires*, 3 vols. (Paris, 1942-47), I, pp. 193 and 247-8; J. P. Allain, *Joseph Caillaux*, pp. 306-8.

[52] Claude Fohlen in *Cambridge Economic History of Europe*, VII, pt. 1, p. 373.

[53] François Caron in Ibid., p. 273.

1864 until 1908, all investments were financed internally by retained profits. Dividends were kept small. Between 1872 and 1914, dividends represented an annual average of 4.70% of revenues, while profits amounted to an annual average of 25.11% of revenues. In spite of major reliance on retained earnings, Allevard resorted to external financing from 1908 to 1912, doubling its equity capital (from 2 to 4 MF) and issuing 2.5 MF worth of bonds. These issues were handled by Banque Charpenay, a private bank in Grenoble, on terms advantageous to Allevard. It is clear that Allevard did not resort to external financing before 1908 by its own choice. For short term credit the firm borrowed in Lyon from the Guerin Bank, and from branches of the Comptoir National d'Escompte and the Société Générale.[54]

Turning to the supply side, the pronouncements of Henri Germain have been given excessive weight and even misinterpreted. The unwillingness of banks to offer long-term credit or to acquire a direct interest in industrial companies with their own funds does not, as we have seen, signify a purely negative role in regard to industrial enterprise, since underwriting of stock and bond issues can fill the same function without endangering a bank's liquidity. The early years of the Crédit Lyonnais and the vicissitudes of banks during the 1870s and 1880s confirmed the cautious attitude of Germain and others of his generation. In the early years of the 20th century a new generation with different views took over, as René Girault has pointed out.[55] For Girault, the generational change is symbolized by the contrast between Henri Germain and Louis Dorizon, who at 36 became the Director-General of the Société Générale in 1896, a post he retained until 1913.[56] Dorizon was particularly interested in metallurgical and mining companies, but from the viewpoint of domestic critics these enterprises had the great defect of being Russian. The attitudes of the new generation were conditioned by the resumption of rapid growth after the relative stagnation of the 1880s and 1890s.

The yardstick against which the performance of the large French banks was measured, both by contemporaries and later scholars, was the large German investment banks. These German *Grossbanken* provided the strong support for German industry that their French counterparts allegedly neglected. The recent work of Richard Tilly shows that the size and visibility of the *Grossbanken* had led to an exaggeration of their role.[57] Even in

---

[54] Pierre Léon, "L'Usine d'Allevard," *Cahiers d'histoire*, VIII (1963), pp. 144-46.

[55] René Girault, 'Portrait de l'Homme d'Affaires Français vers 1914," *Revue d'histoire moderne et contemporaine*, XVI (1969), pp. 329-49.

[56] Ibid., p. 344. Among the new generation who were interested in foreign enterprises were Noetzlin of Paribas and Maurice Rouvier of the Banque Française pour le Commerce et l'Industrie.

[57] Richard H. Tilly, "German Banking, 1850-1914: Development Assistance for the Strong," *Journal of European Economic History*, XV (1986), pp. 113-50.

Germany self-financing remained the predominant source of capital for large listed corporations. New and medium-size enterprises, which included those that were risky and innovative, received no support from the big German banks. Tilly concludes that the *Grossbanken* devoted "their attention and their resources mainly to the support of already strong and large industrial enterprises . . ."[58]

The diverse elements in the coalition against the big banks included industrialists who were unable to obtain adequate financing. Small and medium-size enterprises, especially proprietorships and partnerships, which were essentially family enterprises, could have difficulty in raising long-term capital outside the family circuits. The penchant for secrecy exhibited by many of these enterprises made it difficult for them to borrow at all. Also marginal enterprises, both joint-stock and traditional, facing competition from domestic or foreign rivals with competitive advantages, might experience difficulty in raising funds, the recovery of which appeared questionable. Cheap and readily available capital cannot compensate for locational and other disadvantages, especially as these advantages probably would be available to rivals too. And where large sums were required, family enterprises of all kinds were at a distinct disadvantage compared with corporations. It was natural enough for businessmen experiencing difficulties to blame their plight on the big banks, or on the lack of adequate tariff protection. And deputies, ever sensitive to local needs, were usually willing to carry these complaints to Paris. Ironically, the critics were partially right in the long run. From the vantage point of the Spring of 1914, foreign investment, which paid for itself from the 1880s on, performed a useful service for surplus French capital. But the war and the Bolshevik Revolution destroyed the pre-war liberal economic order, a consequence no one could foresee.

Hardly a year passed without the question of the real or alleged deficiencies of the banking system arising in the Chamber. In February 1907, the socialists in the Chamber, echoing the whole array of Lysis' charges, attacked the banks for channeling French savings into foreign securities, and criticized the government for permitting it to happen. For the banks, according to Gustave Rouanet, who led the attack, the poorer the security, the greater the profits.[59] Among the "doubtful" securities, Russian government bonds were particularly targeted, since they permitted a reactionary government to postpone democratic reform. Albert Willm declared that those who purchased Russian government bonds "would never see their money again."[60] Edouard Aynard, a banker from Lyon, rejected the view that it was

---

[58] Ibid., p. 150.

[59] *Journal officiel*, Chambre des Députes, Débats Parlementaires, séance du 7 fév. 1907, p. 325.

[60] Ibid., séance du 8 fév. 1907, p. 335.

the cupidity of banks which was responsible, charging instead that it was fear of the socialist program which caused capital to flee the country.[61] Caillaux, the Minister of Finance, blamed, in part, the more favorable tax treatment accorded to foreign government bonds over domestic industrial securities. But mainly he defended capital export as necessary to dispose of "excess capital" which had the advantage of stimulating French exports and promoting French foreign policy.[62]

During a debate on tariff policy in 1909, Simon Plissonnier, a self-characterized small businessman, attacked the big banks in the Chamber for not supporting domestic industry.[63] But he also blamed the socialists, estimating that one billion francs emigrated when the income tax was debated. He received some support from the chairman of the tariff committee, L. L. Klotz, who agreed that the big banks should do more for domestic industry, as was the case in Germany.[64] But in the same year, the Minister of Finance defended the patriotism of the banks and praised them for responding "when the government indicated a national interest to be served."[65] In 1912, now the Minister of Finance, Klotz requested that the banks keep the government informed in advance of all foreign loan negotiations. Klotz also cited figures showing a decline in new foreign loan issues over the previous three years and a rise in new domestic industrial issues quoted on the Paris Bourse.[66] In 1913, Minister of Finance Caillaux was attacked by the right-wing deputy Jules Delahaye for his complaisance in permitting foreign loans.[67] But defenses of the banks by high officials could not stem the reform tide. Demands for reform of the banking structure proliferated, including proposals for the creation of new banks to fill the void in the banking structure. Jules Domergue, editor of the protectionist *Réforme Economique* and Jean Codet, president of the Committee of Commerce and Industry in the Chamber proposed that the government take the initiative in creating new banks.[68]

In May 1911, the short-lived government of Ernest Monis, in which Caillaux was Minister of Finance, instituted an extraparliamentary commission "to study the banking structure in France and search for ways to enable it to provide improved credit facilities for both medium and small

---

[61]   Ibid., p. 343.

[62]   Ibid., p. 342.

[63]   Ibid., séance du 1 juillet 1909, pp. 1747-48. Plissonnier was a manufacturer of agricultural machinery in Lyon.

[64]   Ibid., séance du 6 juillet 1909, p. 1839.

[65]   A. Raffalovich, *Le Marché Financier, 1909-1910*, p. 320.

[66]   A. Raffalovich, *Le Marché Financier, 1912-1913*, pp. 367-74.

[67]   *Journal officiel*, Chambre des députes, Débats parlementaires, séance du 11 dec. 1913, pp. 9761-62.

[68]   J. Domergue, *La Question des sociétés de crédit* (1909), pp. 32-33 and 68-69.

commerce and medium and small industry."[69] The commission was composed of bankers, high ranking civil servants, jurists and representatives of chambers of commerce, small businesses, and workers' cooperatives. The work of the commission was apportioned among three subcommittees each of which drafted a report. The first subcommittee, which examined deficiencies in the banking system, found that both the institutions and the resources were lacking.[70] A second subcommittee examined the experience of French and foreign mutual banks in providing credit for small and medium-size businesses, while the third subcommittee was charged with preparing recommendations to correct deficiencies in the banking system. To aid small commerce they proposed the creation of a network of mutual credit banks (*sociétés de cautions mutuelles*) on the local level that would endorse bills (*effets*) presented to them. A set of regional banks (*banques populaires régionales*) would be created whose function would be to discount these bills. At the top there would be a central bank (*Office Central des Banques Populaires*) which would provide the necessary resources for the regional banks. The funds for the central bank would be initially advanced, interest free, by the state, which would control its operation. Eventually, its resources would come from profits.[71]

Aiding small and medium-size industry with long-term loans (1 to 25 years) provided the subcommittee with its most difficult problem, according to its chairman, Alexis Rostand, the president of the Comptoir National d'Escompte. For this task the subcommittee proposed the creation of a two-tiered structure: a central bank (*Etablissement Central*) and a network of regional banks.[72] These banks would lend on the basis of security provided by the borrower. Both the central and regional banks would be constituted as SAs with their resources coming through stock and bond issues. Although ownership of the banks would be private, government consent would be required for the appointment of the president, vice-president and chief operating officer of the central bank. Also three *censeurs* would be appointed by the government to monitor the central bank's operations. On the basis of the commission's recommendations, the government in November 1912 introduced a comprehensive reform bill.[73]

In 1913, the bill emerged with only minor changes from a detailed examination by the commerce committee of the Chamber, accompanied by a long

69 A. Raffalovich, *Le Marché Financier, 1911-1912*, p. 327.
70 Ibid., p. 329.
71 A. Rostand, *Rapport de la troisième sous-commission* (Paris, 1912); Raffalovich, *Le Marché Financier, 1911-1912*, p. 331.
72 Rostand, *Rapport*, pp. 11ff.
73 *Journal officiel*, Chambre des Députes, Documents Parlementaires, session extraordinaire, 1912, Annexe No. 2212, pp. 7-10.

report by Adolphe Landry.[74] Both the *exposé des motifs* of the government bill and the report of the Commerce Committee explicitly accepted the thesis that the large banks had destroyed local banks and created gaps in the banking structure to the detriment of small and medium-size commerce and industry. The Chamber's committee report contended that the existing network of local and regional banks was too limited and possessed insufficient resources for the task. The bill was represented to the Chamber as a modest proposal containing no significant innovation. The proposal to create mutual credit societies and *banques populaires* for short-term credit, for which there was little opposition in any case, followed well-tested practices in both Germany and Italy. Lacking private action, the state had taken the initiative. But the state's role was to be limited to encouraging private initiative by providing an interest free loan of 12 MF, and exoneration from paying certain taxes. Both the government and the committee reports claimed that the bill simply extended to commerce and industry the (much more generously endowed) facilities that already existed for agriculture, which had been created almost twenty years earlier. The proposed institutions to provide long-term credit were, continuing the analogy, similar to the role of the Crédit Foncier for agriculture.

In general, the bill that actually passed in the Chamber was based on the recommendations of the extraparliamentary commission though the structure created for short-term credit was less centralized. The most controversial (and original) part of the bill concerned the creation of banks to provide long-term credit.[75] But this part of the bill raised no objections in the Chamber during the two sessions devoted to discussing the bill.[76] The bill passed on 19 March 1914. However, the Finance Committee of the Senate saw great danger in the creation of banks for long-term credit because the bill failed to provide sufficiently for the safety of bank capital and deposits.[77] Accordingly, the Committee recommended dropping the provisions for long-term credit from the bill. The special Senate committee appointed to consider the Chamber's bill rallied to this position, considering the central bank for long-term credit "as useless and inoperable rather than as dangerous," though a few months earlier it had approved the Chamber's

[74] *Journal officiel*, Chambre des Députes, Documents Parlementaires, 1913, Annexe No. 2590, pp. 175-202 and *Journal officiel*, Chambre des Députes, DP, session extraordinaire, pp. 102-109.

[75] It was argued that they were both dangerous and unnecessary, *e.g.*, A. Raffalovich, *Le Marché financier, 1911-1912*, p. 332, and Albin Huart, *L'Organisation du crédit en France* (Paris, 1913), pp. 336-47.

[76] *Journal officiel*, Chambre des Députes, Débats Parlementaires, 1914, séances du 6 mars, pp. 1371-72; 18 mars, pp. 1726-39; and 19 mars, pp. 1747-60.

[77] *Journal officiel*, Sénat, Documents Parlementaires, 1915, Annexe No. 195, pp. 81-89.

version.[78] The bill, shorn of its long-term credit provisions, finally became law in 1917.[79]

The report of the Senate's Finance Committee noted approvingly the conclusions of a comprehensive investigation into the question of capital export and capital for domestic industry undertaken by a financial journal in 1913.[80] The journal in question was *Finance-Univers*, which over seven issues (February to August, 1913), conducted an *enquête* on the questions, "Can French industry use additional capital? Can the capital be raised?" Recognizing that these were hotly debated questions, the journal sent out questionnaires to the over 9,000 *établissements* employing more than 50 workers, as well as to trade associations. A large number of the responses were published, grouped by industry. Also, a number of politicians across the political spectrum, and economists were invited to contribute.

On the basis of this investigation the journal concluded that: (1) Foreign investment was both inevitable and useful, and that any attempt to curb the "natural play of economic forces" would be ineffective. (2) Large firms were adequately provided with capital. (3) The capacity of France's industry to absorb additional capital was limited by a lack of labor (this was a common complaint), the high cost of coal, social tensions, taxes and a limited market owing to a low birth rate. On the basis of a relatively small number of negative responses, the journal also concluded that some medium-size firms could use additional long-term credit; and short-term credit should be made available to small producers to finance exports.[81] Historians are generally well advised if they heed informed contemporary opinion.

[78] *Journal officiel*, Sénat, Documents Parlementaires, 1915, Annexe No. 307, supplementary report of the Senate Committee, p. 205.
[79] On the background of these mutual banks, see Sylvie Boudoulec, "Les Banques populaires des origines à la loi de 1917," *Revue de l'économie sociale*, V (1985), pp. 17-24.
[80] *Journal officiel*, Sénat, Documents Parlementaires, 1915, Annexe No. 195, p. 83.
[81] *Finance-Univers*, 15 Aug. 1913, pp. 5-12.

CHAPTER IV

FINANCING INDUSTRIAL CORPORATIONS

*Les capitaux ne font pas défaut à l'industrie, mais qu'au
contraire l'industrie fait souvent défaut aux capitaux*

Albert Thomas, 1913

In addition to separating ownership and management and spreading risks, the corporate form of business organization permits large sums of capital to be raised. Whether or not corporations can readily raise needed funds affects the pace of economic change. Availability of capital is crucial to company promotion. Once a corporation has commenced operation, three methods of raising additional capital, at least in theory, are available: (1) reinvesting profits, (2) borrowing from banks, and (3) the issue of additional stocks, or bonds. Much has been written about the difficulty of raising capital by French corporations; and it is generally alleged that self-financed investment was practiced of necessity, often because the big banks declined to lend their support.

Generally, self-financing of new investment from current or past profits was regarded as the optimal method, not only for family firms, but also for corporations whose ownership was widely diffused. Dealing with banks for other than short-term financing necessitated admitting bank representatives to the board of directors. Debt was an addition to fixed costs, which mortgaged future profits and reduced financial flexibility. Banks also could be fair weather friends, supportive during good times, but unreliable when the economic climate deteriorated. Likewise, even when the option of issuing securities was readily available, self-financing was generally preferable: bonds added to fixed costs, and additional stock diluted equity. Self-financing was a tradition, a recognized embodiment of best practice, though for some enterprises at certain times it was also a necessity. This predilection for self-financing was reinforced by a generation of entrepreneurs who experienced the depression of the 1880s and early 1890s.

However, notwithstanding these attitudes toward self-financing, historians have exaggerated the reliance on self-financing and ignored the choice which corporate enterprises often enjoyed between using retained earnings or issuing securities.[1] There were also forces which pushed corporations to utilize the capital market. Corporate management was subject to stockholder pressures to pay larger dividends; and a good dividend record was a *sine qua non* for the issue of additional stock. Corporations in which banks took an active role might favor resorting to the capital market to collect underwriting fees. For proprietorships and partnerships, the option of issuing securities did not exist; aside from borrowing from banks or individuals, these enterprises were forced to rely upon self-financing. For the period 1900-1913 we have the estimates of G. F. Teneul for the annual average investment of enterprises:

Table 4.1   Annual Average Investment of Enterprises, 1900-1913

Self-financing of individual enterprises	600 MF
Self-financing of corporate enterprises	1,000 MF
Financing through the issue of securities	650 MF
TOTAL INVESTMENT	2,250 MF

Source: Georges Francois Teneul, *Le Financement des entreprises en France* (Paris, 1961), pp. 106-110.

For corporate enterprises, Teneul estimates the annual average investment for the period at 1,650 MF, of which 1,000 MF came from retained earnings and 650 MF from the capital market. The margin of error for these estimates, as Tenuel admits, is large. Even so, they show that 40% of corporate investment was financed by the capital market.

Aggregates and averages tend to obscure many of the complexities of corporate finance which depended upon many variables: general economic conditions, the size of the firm, the personality of managers, the degree of risk and the sector of industry. New unproven industries, old declining industries and youthful expanding industries cannot be lumped together. Though they further our understanding, global statistics for the respective shares of self financing, bank loans (even if they were available, and they

---

[1]   *E.g.*, "... l'autofinancement n'est à aucun degré le lot exclusif des firmes de petit ou de moyenne envergure au XIXe siècle. Il est aussi la loi des grandes entreprises par actions, et des grosses sociétés en commandite. S'il fallait chercher une constant (dans le temps et dans l'espace) du développement industriel européen du siècle passé, c'est la *pratique de l'autofinancement maximum* qui nous la fournirait le plus visiblement." Jean Bouvier, "Rapports entre systèmes bancaires et entreprises industrielles dans la croissance Européenne au XIXe siècle," Pierre Léon *et al.*, *L'Industrialisation en Europe au XIXe siècle* (Paris, 1973) p. 119.

are not), and the issue of securities, obscure the problems of differing sectors and firms. An examination of selected sectors and individual firms helps to bring into focus decisions regarding corporate finance.

Iron and Steel

The iron and steel sector is said to be characterized by heavy reliance on self-financing.[2] This sector was undergoing major technological change during the last quarter of the 19th century in which the shift from iron to steel required huge investments. Problems of technology were compounded by a slow growing or stagnant market between 1875 and 1895, and difficulties of access to raw materials. Generally, production in the iron and steel industry coincided with the performance of the industrial sector as a whole. Crouzet's general index of French industrial production shows the period 1875 to 1895 to be one of slow growth: generally stagnant for the years 1875-1879, 1884-1888 and 1893-1895, but interspersed with short spurts of growth in 1880-1883 and 1889-1892.[3] After 1895 the picture improves with periods of slow growth alternating with periods of rapid growth until 1914.

The Franco-Prussian War, 1870-1871, and the loss of territory to Germany by the Treaty of Frankfurt, interrupted the growth in pig iron production (See Table 4.2). The de Wendel firm which passed into Germany in 1871 alone accounted for more than 10% of French production in 1869. Nonetheless, after a small decline for the period 1870-1874, growth resumed, bouyed in the early 1880s by the Freycinet Plan, which provided the industry with huge orders for railroad construction. Production declined during the period 1885-1889, but resumed in the 1890s and continued, with increasing momentum, until the outbreak of the war. Thus, the first decade, 1875-1884 was one of growth, the second decade, 1885-1894, one of depression and recovery. What accounts for the depressed years of 1885-1889 and the relatively slow growth during the period 1890-1894?

[2] *E.g.*, Clement Colson, *Cours d'économic politique*, 5 vols. (Paris, 1901-1907), III, p. 345; Ann Wendy Mill, "French Steel and Metal-Working Industries: A Contribution to Debate on Economic Development in Nineteenth Century France," *Social Science History*, IX (1985), pp. 330-33.
[3] François Crouzet, "Essai de construction d'un indice annuel de la production industrielle française au XIXe siècle." *Annales: Economies, Sociétés, Civilisations*, vol. 25 (1970), p. 96.

Table 4.2 Annual Average Pig Iron Production

Years	Thousands of metric tons	Years	Thousands of metric tons
1860-64	1,065	1890-94	1,998
1865-69	1,261	1895-99	2,386
1870-74	1,211	1900-04	2,665
1875-79	1,462	1905-09	3,390
1880-84	1,918	1910-13	4,664
1885-89	1,627		

Source: *Annuaire Statistique de la France*, annual volumes.

Two major challenges confronted the French iron and steel industry during the 1880s. One was a drastic drop in demand for rails and railroad equipment after 1885, the other stemmed from the invention of the Gilchrist-Thomas dephosphorization process. These challenges closely followed the problems posed by the introduction of steelmaking, particularly the Bessemer process, between 1865 and 1875. The major area of concentration of the French metallurgical industry, the upper Rhône and Loire valleys (the Center), rested upon a declining resource base ill-suited to the new steel technology. The investment requirements were huge and raised questions about ultimate profitability. But after some initial hesitation, French firms embarked on the manufacture of steel, using both Bessemer converters and open hearth (Siemens-Martin) furnaces.[4] Since the Bessemer process required pure iron ore not obtainable locally, Algerian iron ore provided the basis for the introduction of the steel industry in the Center. Many companies explored the possibility of Sardinia and Spain as additional or alternate sources of ore to the Mokta el Hadid mines of Algeria.[5] Although the Center continued as the focal point of the iron and steel industry, new furnaces were constructed on the Mediterranean coast, on the banks of the Rhône, and on the Atlantic coast to utilize Algerian and foreign ore.

The depression of the 1880s had little affect on the iron and steel industry until after 1885 when the termination of the Freycinet plan ended new construction. Steel rails alone accounted for more than 70% of finished steel products (*acier fondu*) during the decade 1875-1884 (See Table 4.3). Steel rail production dropped from an annual average of 323,000 tons for the period 1880-1884, to 226,000 tons for the period 1885-1889 and to 202,000

4 Bertrand Gille, *La Sidérurgie française au XIXe siècle* (Geneva, 1968), p. 256.
5 Ibid., p. 259.

tons for the period 1890-1894. Since steel rails lasted ten times longer than iron rails (and cost only about 25% more) replacement orders were less frequent.[6] The demand for other finished steel products for railroads, such as wheel rims, journal boxes, and axels also declined. Nevertheless, even with the drastic decline in domestic railroad orders after 1884, steel production continued to grow, with steel rails accounting for an ever decreasing portion of total steel production. As production of steel rails declined, the slack was more than taken up by the expansion of new markets for steel products.

Table 4.3   Production of Finished Steel Products
(thousands of metric tons)

Annual Average	Total Production	Rails	% Rails
1875-1879	283	205	72%
1880-1884	459	323	70%
1885-1889	504	226	45%
1890-1894	648	202	31%
1899	1,240	256	21%
1913	3,186	461	11%

Source: *Annuaire Statistique de la France*, annual volumes.

Technological change and access to raw materials caused a geographical shift in the industry from the Center (upper Loire valley) to the rich iron ore deposits of the East (Meurthe et Moselle Department) and, to a lesser extent, to the coal mines of the North (Nord and Pas de Calais Departments). This shift was abetted by the invention of the Gilchrist-Thomas process, which permitted the use of the minette ores of the Lorraine for steelmaking. The iron and steel industry of the Center could not compete with industry based upon either the cheap pig iron of the East or the less expensive coal of the North. It survived, taking advantage of a modern plant and a skilled work force, by concentrating on high grade steel, and on finished iron and steel products.

The East accounted for 25% of the pig iron produced in France in 1877; twenty years later it produced 62% of France's pig iron (See Table 4.4). This is all the more remarkable when one takes into account the growth in total production. The East was well situated for the production of Thomas steel, but steelmaking lagged until 1893 because of the refusal of de Wendel to

---

[6]   François Caron, "Les Commandes des compagnies de chemin de fer en France de 1850 à 1914," *Revue d'histoire de la Sidérurgie*, VI (1965), p. 151.

share patent rights to the process with other producers.[7] Thereafter production of steel in the East expanded rapidly, accounting for 54% of total production by 1913. Lacking coal, the East depended upon the North, Belgium, and Westphalia for its coke. The North retained its share of pig iron production, but the ore came from outside the region. However, its share of the ferrous metal working industry expanded, relying in part on Eastern pig iron.

Table 4.4   Geographical Distribution of Pig Iron Production
(thousands of metric tons)

Year	Nord and Pas de Calais	% of total production	Meurthe et Moselle	% of total production	% rest of France
1877	228	15	383	25	60
1881	275	15	538	29	56
1885	311	19	707	43	38
1888	317	19	911	54	27
1893	285	14	1,216	61	25
1897	377	15	1,546	62	23
1901	349	15	1,446	61	24
1905	389	13	2,109	69	18
1909	540	15	2,429	68	17
1913	933	18	3,493	67	15

Source: *Annuaire Statistique de la France*, annual volumes.

The Center declined, first in the production of pig iron, then steel and finally in metal working. Many of the Center's firms expanded into the East to assure themselves of supplies of pig iron and steel. The period 1875-1895 was a transitional period for the French iron and steel industry during which the groundwork was laid for the rapid expansion that took place after 1895. With the exception of the latter 1880s, the industry grew, rapidly in the early 80s, less so in the late 70s and early 90s. It faced some handicaps, particularly the cost of coal. France's major coal and iron ore deposits were geographically separated. With the increasing efficiency of furnaces during the 19th century, the advantage of transporting ore, particularly low grade ore, to fuel disappeared, but the problem of the **cost** of coal remained. France

---

[7]   Claude Beaud, "Schneider, de Wendel et les brevets Thomas," *Cahiers d'histoire* 9 (1975), p. 376; Anthony Rowley, *Evolution économique de la France du milieu du XIXe siècle à 1914* (Paris, 1982), p. 342.

normally had to import approximately one-third of the coal it consumed. The overall quality of the coal from its own Northern basin was inferior to that of the Ruhr. Costs of transport of coal, or coke, were significant. An official inquiry in 1919 placed the part of fuel in 1913 in the cost of production of a ton of French pig iron at 36% of the total, but only 22% for Germany and 20% for Great Britain.[8] This difference cannot be attributed to technological inferiority. In 1913, French producers paid 22% more for a ton of coal than their German counterparts.[9] Although these figures are for 1913, they are indicative of the problem of coal costs faced by French industrialists throughout the period.

Brief case histories involving the financing of four iron and steel companies follow. Alais, Chatillon-Commentry, Nord-Est, and the Aciéries de Longwy were selected, instead of others, because of the existence of easily accessible fairly complete runs of company annual reports, for geographical balance, and because each company is significantly different from the others. Unfortunately the financial information is far from complete, particularly in regard to bank loans, which are often concealed in the financial statements under such vague headings as "diverse creditors."

Alais was a firm, like those of the Center, which was increasingly beset with problems of access to raw materials. Founded as an SA in 1830 and located in the Gard Department about mid-way between Lyon and Marseille, the company was an important producer of rails during the early railway age. It was an integrated company with its own coal and iron ore mines — in fact, the coal mine dominated the company. By the end of the Second Empire, the local iron ore mines were approaching exhaustion and the company was forced to seek its ore outside the Department, from the Aude, the Pyrenees and from Spain. The prospects were such that the Board of Directors refused to contemplate the needed investment for Alais to engage in the manufacture of steel, at a time when the railroads were already turning to steel rails. Under these circumstances, in 1874, the company was happy to lease for twenty years the metallurgical portion of its business to the Terrenoire Company, which planned to construct a Martin furnace for steelmaking.[10] A guaranteed return of 5% on the factory was deemed better than the risks of large additional investments, or renouncing the rail business to concentrate on the manufacture of wrought iron. At the end of the lease, they hoped to recover the factory in better shape than at the beginning.

The bankruptcy of Terrenoire forced Alais to resume control of the factory

---

[8] F. Caron, "La Croissance industrielle. secteurs et branches," in Braudel, Fernand and Ernest Labrousse, eds., *Histoire économique et social de la France*, IV, i (1978), p. 299.

[9] Rowley, *Evolution économique*, p. 331.

[10] For the history of the Alais Company to 1875, see Robert R. Locke, *Les Fonderies et Forges d'Alais a l'époque des premiers chemins de fer, 1829-1874.*

in 1884, well before the expiration of the lease. In 1886 the company resorted to the capital market issuing 2 MF of 5% bonds for new investment and working capital.[11] Alais also omitted dividends from 1885 through 1888. Another issue of bonds for 2.65 MF at 4% occurred in 1893, the proceeds of which were used to retire the remainder of the 1885 bonds (1.89 MF) with the remainder divided between new investments and working capital. From 1885 to 1905 the company largely relied on retained earnings to satisfy its modest capital outlays. From being among the most important firms in the industry during the Second Empire, its status was now marginal. But in the last decade before the war there was a serious attempt to modernize and for this reliance upon retained earnings was not possible.

Shortly after the turn of the century Alais' problems became critical. It required large new capital outlays without the earnings to finance them. The company opted, in 1905, to take advantage of the new laws facilitating the issue of preferred shares by issuing 3.5 MF of preferred shares with the right to a 4% cumulative dividend. These shares were to be gradually amortized. By 1909 the major factory at Tamaris received more than 4 MF in improvements. New capital requirements continued at a high level. In 1909, an additional 4 MF of 4.5% bonds were issued, followed in 1912 by the issue of 30,000 new regular shares at 250 francs for a total of 7.5 MF. In 1909 bonds were the choice since the dividend on ordinary shares was omitted for fiscal 1907-1908. In 1912, when dividends on ordinary shares had risen to 10 francs, the decision was to increase equity.

Thus between 1905 and 1914, Alais raised 14.5 MF on the capital market, more than triple its nominal capital. Additional funds came from retained earnings. For the four years 1907-1908 to 1910-1911, net profits amounted to almost 4.8 MF, of which only one-quarter were distributed to stockholders. Apart from short-term credit, the main contribution of banks appears to have been to facilitate access to the capital market. Its connections with banks appear to have become increasingly close. In 1912 of the twelve man board of directors, Alais shared directors with 5 banks: the Banque Privé Lyon-Marseille, which was the underwriter of the 1909 bond issue, the Caisse Commerciale et Industrielle de Paris, the Banque de l'Union Parisienne, Neuflize et Cie., and the Omnium Lyonnais.

The Chatillon-Commentry Company offers an example of the efficacy of retained earnings to provide for its financial needs.[12] Created by the merger of two existing firms as a CPA in 1845, it finally received authorization as an SA in 1862 after two unsuccessful attempts.[13] It was capitalized at 12.5 MF. During the late 1860s and early '70s, the company acted aggressively to

11 AN, 65AQ, K3[1-2], Fonderies et Forges d'Alais.
12 AN, 65 AQ, K46[1-2], Forges de Chatillon-Commentry.
13 C. Freedeman, *Joint-Stock Enterprise*, pp. 76-77, 119-20.

maintain its position among France's largest producers, embarking on a program of modernizing its facilities and acquiring coal mines.[14] As a firm located in the Center region, it suffered from lack of access to raw materials, which it attempted to alleviate first by building blast furnaces at Beaucaire in the lower Rhône for easy access to the high grade ores of Algeria and Spain,[15] and in 1880 by purchasing Villerupt in the East, soon to become the dominant region for iron and steel production. Villerupt was acquired to provision the factories of the Center region, but transport costs from Villerupt to the company's main factory at Montlucon ran 19 francs a ton.

In 1895 the company opened negotiations with a large Eastern firm, the Société Métallurgique de Champigneulles et Neuves-Maisons for a merger which was achieved in 1897, with the stockholders of Champigneulles receiving 6 MF of shares in Chatillon-Commentry, raising the nominal capitalization of the company to 18.5 MF.[16] Champigneulles brought to the company rich iron mines and four blast furnaces, with a fifth under construction. It had the additional merit of being only one-half the distance as Villerupt from the company's refining and metalworking operations in the Allier Department, providing an assured source for pig iron. The company embarked on a huge plan for new investment, involving the construction of two additional blast furnaces and a steel mill, which proved beyond its capacity to finance from retained earnings. In 1900 the company issued 15 MF of 4% bonds, the only time the company was to enter the capital market from the time it became an SA in 1862 and 1914. The company continued to invest heavily in the pre-war years, to build up large capital reserves, to amortize its bonded indebtedness (only 4.5 MF of the 1900 loan remained in 1914), and to increase its dividends (from 50 francs a year for the period 1899-1905 to 85 francs for 1913 and 1914). The company paid dividends without interruption beginning in 1864. Given its policy of self-financing, dividends were frugal. From 1895 to 1911, only about one-third of profits were distributed as dividends.

Company financial statements are generally silent on the use of bank credit for working capital, but other sources provide some indications. Bertrand Gille has found that Chatillon-Commentry was able to borrow 740,000 francs from a dozen local bankers in the early 1870s.[17] This is not unusual. Some companies, in the late 1860s and early 1870s, notably Le Creusot, Fourchambault and Chatillon-Commentry, acted as their own banks by accepting deposits.[18] The Terrenoire Company accepted demend

---

[14] B. Gille, *La Sidérurgie française*, p. 260.

[15] Ibid., p. 261.

[16] Since its shares of 500 francs nominal value were selling at 780 on the Bourse, the company's market capitalization was more than 50% higher.

[17] Gille, *La Sidérurgie française*, p. 265.

[18] Ibid., p. 264.

deposits bearing 5% interest from its employees and administrators, which, by the 1880s, amounted to a virtual long term loan of 5 MF.[19] Chatillon-Commentry changed the rate of interest on its deposits according to their monetary needs. This practice probably did not survive, but it is one which played an important role in some companies during the 19th century. In general, companies could rely upon credit from their suppliers, or credit accounts (*comptes courants*) from banks on which they could draw for short-term funds.

The Forges et Aciéries du Nord et de l'Est affords a contrast to those firms which relied primarily upon self-financing in three respects: (1) its close ties with banks, (2) its extensive use of the capital market, and (3) its generous dividend policy.[20] Organized in 1881, it was the product of a merger between the Mines et Usines du Nord et de l'Est, founded in 1873 by Adolphe Leclercq as an SA, and the Eastern (Meurthe et Moselle Department) pig iron producer Steinbach et Cie.. The Mines et Usines du Nord et de l'Est, as its name indicates, already possessed an iron mine and smelting facility in the East to help provide its factories at Valenciennes (Nord Department) with pig iron, but the merger with Steinbach et Cie. greatly strengthened the company's resource base. Both before and after the merger, the Mines et Usines du Nord et d'Est was supported by French (Paribas) and Belgian banking interests, who were represented on the board. The new company was capitalized nominally at 12 MF (about 6 MF in actuality), with 24,000 shares of 500 francs (nominal). 8,000 shares went to the shareholders of the Mines et Usines du Nord et de l'Est, 7,500 to Steinbach et Cie. and the remaining 8,500 for cash at 250 francs each. Expanding its steelmaking capacity necessitated large capital expenditures. In 1883 the company issued 2 MF of 5% bonds. From 1882 to 1889 it used bank credit extensively, the amount owed on *comptes courants* on June 30th running between 2.3 MF (1885) and 4 MF (1883). In the 1890s, these sums declined.

After the turn of the century, it became necessary to raise huge sums to develop a new iron mine at Pienne in the East, and to build a large modern integrated steel mill in the North. The practice of bringing pig iron from the East to be reheated and processed in the North was not economical as it required a double expenditure for fuel. For the new integrated plant, the iron ore would be shipped to Valenciennes to be processed directly into steel products. Construction of the expensive new plant at Valenciennes, which began in 1903, necessitated a capital outlay of 38 MF by 1913, and development of the iron ore mine at Pienne cost an additional 13 MF. About two-thirds of these expenditures were raised on the capital market: 9 MF by

[19] Pierre Cayez, *Crises et croissance de l'industrie lyonnaise, 1850-1900* (Paris, 1980), p. 214.
[20] AN 65AQ, K159[1-2], Forges et Aciéries du Nord et de l'Est.

the issue of 6,000 additional shares of stock (at 1,520 francs a share) in 1906, and two issues of bonds for 10 MF each in 1909 and 1910 and a final 5 MF in 1914 for a total of 34 MF.

The company maintained high dividends during the period of heavy investment: Dividends rose from 80 francs a share in 1903 to 85 in 1907 to 90 in 1912. Beginning in 1886, the company paid dividends every year until the war, a total of more than 45 MF. In addition several million was paid to the members of the board of directors, who were each entitled to 1% of the net profits after the stockholders received 5% on their shares, and a 5% levy for the legal reserve.

The Aciéries de Longwy, an Eastern company, is similar to Nord-Est in its reliance upon the capital market for its new investment and its maintenance of high dividends, but although it early had recourse to bank loans, unlike Nord-Est, control remained firmly in the hands of ironmasters.[21] The Aciéries de Longwy, founded as an SA in 1880, united the operations of two ironmaster families: the Labbés at Mont Saint-Martin and the d'Adelswards at Prieure, each having three blast furnaces. The company erected a Bessemer converter using the Thomas process in 1883 and added an open-hearth (Thomas) furnace in 1890. By 1914 the company was integrated with its own iron and coal mines. In partnership with the important German firm of Gebrüder Roechling, each owned half interest in the Karl Alexander coal mine in Germany and in the iron mine at Valleroy in French Lorraine. After early management problems, the firm came under the direction in 1888 of Alexandre Dreux, the former director of the Comptoir de Longwy, who remained in control for almost forty years.

Capitalized initially at 15 MF, the company also had a bonded indebtedness of 3.25 MF at the time of its founding. The first decade of the company's operations were difficult. Capital expenditures were high and profits were too low to cover capital expenditures. The company omitted dividend payments in 1883-1884 (1 July–30 June) and from 1886-1887 through 1889-1890. To raise money, the company issued 1.75 MF of bonds in 1882-1883; it increased its capitalization to 20 MF in 1883-1884 by issuing 5 MF worth of new shares; and it secured a long-term bank loan of 1.5 MF. (Unfortunately, the financial statements do not give further details.) The company's financial statement shows short-term bank debt (notes and *comptes courants*) of almost 2 MF in 1889-1890.

The decade of the 1890s was prosperous. The company reduced its bonded indebtedness to about 1 MF, paid off its long-term bank debt, built up its reserve funds to 4 MF, and resumed the payment of dividends, which totaled 14.2 MF from 1890-1891 to 1899-1900.

After 1900, capital expenditures soared, totaling more than 70 MF for the

21 AN 65AQ, K123[1-3], Aciéries de Longwy.

period 1900-1901 to 1912-1913. More than half of these expenditures were met by the issue of new securities. The company issued bonds for 16.5 MF between 1902 and 1912 (3 MF in 1902, 2.5 MF in 1908, 6 MF in 1910 and 5 MF in 1912) and additional shares of stock for 21 MF (8,000 shares at 750 francs in 1903 and 12,000 shares at 1,250 francs in 1914) for a total of 37.5 MF. Dividend payments for the period from 1900-1901 to 1912-1913 were more than 29 MF with an additional approximately 5 MF going to members of the board. The board was entitled to 10% of the profits after 5% was levied for the legal reserve and the shareholders had received 5% on their shares. In 1907, the 7 members of the board split 639,000 francs. The Aciéries de Longwy illustrates the willingness of businessmen to resort to both banks and the capital market in the troubled 1880s, and to the capital market in the boom years preceding the war. If these examples represent a fair sample, as I believe they do, the alleged forced reliance of French iron and steel corporations on self-financing is a myth. A brief examination of corporations in other sectors of the economy affords additional perspectives on the question of corporate finance.

Mining

The Carmaux coal mining company, long a partnership controlled by the local de Solages family was acquired by Parisian financial interests in 1856. It was founded first as a CPA pending its authorization as an SA, which occurred only in 1860.[22] No nominal value was assigned to its 23,200 shares, but the average market value of its shares on the Paris Bourse in 1860 was 7.3 MF. Located in the south of France, the company enjoyed prosperity even though its extraction costs were relatively high (as compared with the Nord and Pas de Calais), because its markets were protected by high transport costs. The company's only recourse to the capital market occurred in 1858 shortly after its formation as a CPA with a bond issue of 3.25 MF (nominal). Although the company experienced serious financial constraints in the 1860s, rising profits in the 1870s made it relatively easy for the company to meet its financial requirements from retained earnings.

In 1870 the company extracted 139,000 tons; its production gradually increased to 664,000 tons by 1913. Dividends were paid continuously, averaging 20 francs per share for the period 1860-1870, 70.5 francs per share for 1871-1880, 74.5 francs per share for 1881-1890, 54.5 francs per share for 1891-1900 and 96.8 francs per share for 1901-1913. The company

22 AN 65AQ, L83[1-2], Société des Mines de Carmaux. An excellent sketch of the company's history may be found in Rolande Trempe, *Les Mineurs de Carmaux, 1848-1914*, 2 vols. (Paris, 1971), I, pp. 21-103.

met its investment needs and at the same time paid high dividends. Net profits for 1893-1913 totalled 58.2 MF, 66.5% of which were paid as dividends (38.7 MF). Certainly the Carmaux company was not forced to rely upon retained earnings for its financial needs, but did so by choice.

The Société des Mines de Lens offers a similar example.[23] Exploiting one of the new concessions in the Pas de Calais, the company was founded in 1855 as a *société civile*, capitalized at 3 MF. As a *société civile*, the company escaped the provisions of the *Code de Commerce* and the 1867 law, thus it was not required to publish financial statements. From the start, control remained in the hands of a number of local families. It expanded production rapidly, from almost 100,000 tons in 1860 to over 4,000,000 tons in 1912-1913 (1 August–31 July), accounting in the pre-war years, for about 10% of total French production. In 1912 the company employed over 16,000 workers and provided more than 7,000 houses and gardens for its employees. Except for an issue of bonds for 3 MF in 1893, and not excluding possible bank loans from time to time, it satisfied its capital requirements from retained earnings.

The Aniche company is yet another example of a coal mine that, with one important exception, met its financial needs through retained earnings.[24] An old mine in the Nord Department, the company was founded in 1773, and like Lens, escaped both the provisions of the *Code de Commerce* and the law of 1867. Its production was small until the Second Empire. Between 1898 and 1906 it floated three bond issues totaling 16 MF (4 MF in 1898, 6 MF in 1904 and 6 MF in 1906) in order to expand its production, which approximately doubled. By 1913, Aniche employed about 10,000 workers and extracted 2.45 million tons of coal. The example of Aniche suggests that for a solid company there was no difficulty in raising large sums, if the company chose to do so.

Engineering

The cases of the Anciens Etablissements Cail/SFCM and of Fives-Lille, two engineering firms, highlight the effects of declining railroad orders, particularly after the completion of the Freycinet Plan in the mid-1880s.[25] As major manufacturers of railroad equipment, they were both dependent upon a market that until the mid-1880s was fueled by new construction and replacement orders. The first virtually came to a halt and the second

23 AN 65AQ, L248, Société des Mines de Lens.
24 AN 65AQ, L33, Aniche.
25 F. Caron, "Les Commandes des compagnies de chemins de fer en France," pp. 148-49.

declined. The question of what would replace, if anything, the declining domestic railroad market became a question of crucial importance.

For the SA des Anciens Etablissements Cail,[26] the manufacture of armaments appeared to be the means of salvation during a difficult period. Attempts by outsiders like Cail to enter the field were risky, for it meant breaking into the ranks of entrenched suppliers. An old company, founded in 1812, J. F Cail et Cie. was a partnership (*commandite simple*) from 1850 to 1870, when it was transformed into a CPA. When J. F. Cail died the following year he was succeeded by his son as *gérant*. The company fared poorly. There were no dividends paid from 1875 to 1882. Reorganized as an SA in 1882 under the auspices of Paris and Lyon banking and financial interests, during a period that one disaffected stockholder later called a "time of illusions," the company was capitalized at 20 MF. Within a few years, the company moved, under its director, a well known artillery officer, Colonel de Bange, to replace declining railroad orders with the manufacture of artillery, though machinery to distill alcohol, refine sugar, and bridges were not neglected.

Unfortunately, orders for Cail's newly developed canons were scarce, with just a small order from Serbia. After three years without dividends, and the loss of about half of the company's capital, the stockholders revolted, voting out the colonel and the board of directors, amid press reports that German and Jewish bankers, acting as agents of Bismarck, were trying to destroy a competitor of Krupp. In spite of strong sentiment to wind up the company or merge it with Fives-Lille (negotiations in 1889 and 1890 failed to produce an agreement) the company continued with its capital reduced to 10 MF. After paying dividends of 20 francs per share for three years (1890-1892), it omitted dividends over the next five years. The company's financial statements for 1894 and 1895 show a loan of 2 MF from the Crédit Foncier de France.

The company was reorganized in 1898 as the Société Française des Constructions Mécaniques (SFCM), shifting its manufacturing operations from Paris to Denain (Nord) in closer proximity to supplies of coal and pig iron. Capitalized at 8 MF, the holders of Cail shares received 5 MF in stock in the new SFCM, plus the proceeds from the sale of land and factories in Paris (perhaps another 250 francs per share). A prime mover in the reorganization was the Lyon financier Jean Bonnardel. SFCM resorted to the capital market issuing shares for 4 MF in 1899 and 6 MF in 1912, the first issue at a slight premium and the second a premium of 200 francs. The two issues yielded almost 15 MF. In the last few years before the outbreak of the war, the company enjoyed its greatest prosperity. This company was largely at

[26] AN 65 AQ, M82-83, Anciens Etablissements Cail/Société Française des Constructions Mécaniques.

the mercy of the vageries of demand for its products, and pressure for new investment was present only when demand for its products was high. Certainly, the company would have experienced great difficulty raising funds on the capital market during the frequent periods when dividends were omitted, but at those times there was little incentive for the company to invest.

The Fives-Lille Company, founded as an SARL in 1866 as a successor to the CPA parent, Schaken, Caillet et Cie., was primarily a producer of railroad equipment.[27] Two years later, taking advantage of the 1867 law, it transformed itself into an SA. The first decade of the company's operations were prosperous, both profits and dividends were high. From 1875-1876 (1 July–30 June) to 1896-1897, profits were modest and dividends fell from between 70 and 100 francs to 30 and 35. More successfully than Cail, at least for a time, it survived the end of the Freycinet Plan. When faced with declining orders for locomotives and railroad equipment, Fives-Lille diversified into other product lines (hydraulic lifts, electric cranes, equipment for electric power stations and tramways), and into large public works projects, particularly railroads, in foreign countries; attempts by the firm to enter the arms business met with little success.[28]

One characteristic of companies like Fives-Lille was that their customers expected them to provide medium-term, and even long-term, credit, or to accept stock in the customer's company as payment. This resulted in a large number of bad debts. The company established a special fund in the 1860s, dubbed the "Ducroire Fund," as a reserve to cover such debts. As suppliers of sugar refining equipment, Fives-Lille became a sugar refiner in the 1880s by falling heir to three bankrupt sugar refining companies. These were spun off as a separate SA in 1900, before they were ultimately absorbed by the Raffineries et Sucreries Say in 1905. More serious was the financial disaster resulting from the company's involvement in the building of the Spanish Southern Railroad (Linares to Almeria), when the railroad company and the Spanish government defaulted on payments due the company. Demonstrating the perils of foreign markets, this loss of over 5 MF caused dividends to be omitted for ten years. After surmounting this crisis, from 1908 on, the company participated fully in the pre-war boom.

Fives-Lille was a company with a high dividend pay-out ratio. From 1867-1868 until dividends were omitted after 1896-1897, dividends totalled over 23 MF. To this may be added several millions for the board of directors and bonuses to key personnel. Dividends and other emoluments probably

---

[27] AN 65AQ, M200, Fives-Lille. See also François Crouzet, "When the Railways Were Built, A French Engineering Firm during the 'Great Depression' and After," in Sheila Marriner, ed., *Business and Businessmen* (Liverpool, 1978), pp. 105-139.

[28] François Crouzet, "When the Railways Were Built," pp. 114-15.

amounted to more than three-quarters (the financial statements do not permit a precise calculation) of net profits. When dividends were resumed after 1907-1908, the pay-out ratio was much smaller. François Crouzet has calculated that only 28% of net profits for the seven year period from 1907-1908 to 1913-1914 were distributed.[29] After the near fatal experience with Spanish railroads, building up large reserves of cash and faster depreciation became the order of the day.

Given the high pay-out ratio for much of its history, it is not surprising that the company resorted frequently to the capital market for funds, the total amounting to 36.5 MF from 1867 to 1914: Two bond issues of 6 MF each, the first in 1867 to provide working capital, and the second in 1878. In 1880 the company doubled its capitalization by issuing 6 MF of new stock. In 1897 it tapped the bond market for 12.5 MF to help it survive its financial crisis, and in 1914 it realized 6 MF from a new stock issue. Neither of the quite different experiences of Cail/SFCM nor Fives-Lille fit the stereotype of companies forced to rely on retained earnings for their capital requirements.

Electricity and Gas

In the last two decades preceding the outbreak of the war, the new electrical industry was growing rapidly with companies appearing to generate and supply electric power for urban communities, build and operate tramways and underground railroads, and to supply equipment of all types. The huge amounts of capital required made this industry one of the key contributors in creating and sustaining the long pre-war boom.[30]

The Compagnie Française Thomson-Houston, organized in 1893 and capitalized initially at 1 MF, employed General Electric patents from which the company derived its name.[31] At first it specialized in the building of tramways, but later broadened its activities as a manufacturer of electrical equipment. Since it partially financed the construction of tramways by taking shares in the lines it constructed, it was, in effect, a trust for the shares of other enterprises. Usually between one-half to two-thirds of its assets consisted of the shares of other companies. Under the circumstances, its capital requirements were enormous. To meet its needs, Thomson-Houston relied primarily upon the capital market. It increased its capital by stages from 1 MF in 1893 to 5 MF in 1894, to 15 MF in 1896 (the issue of the

[29] Ibid., pp. 123-24.
[30] Maurice Lévy-Leboyer, "Le Système électrique en France, 1880-1940," *Revue française de gestion*, No. 70 (Sept.–Oct. 1988), pp. 88-99.
[31] AN 65AQ, G602$^{1-2}$, Compagnie Française Thomson-Houston.

additional 10 MF of shares at a 250 francs premium netted 15 MF), to 25 MF in 1897 (again at a premium of 250 francs for a net of 15 MF), to 40 MF in 1898 (once again at a premium of 250 francs for at net of 22.5 MF) and finally to 60 MF in 1909 (only a little more than one-third of the 1909 issue was marketed, the premium of which was 150 francs, and the rest going to shareholders of companies being absorbed by Thomson-Houston). Total additions to capital by the issue of stock from 1894 to 1909 came to 82.5 MF including premiums. Bond issues totaled 55 MF (nominal — the net to the company being between 3 to 9% lower): 10 MF in 1896, 20 MF in 1899, 10 MF in 1908 and 15 MF in 1913.

Thomson-Houston paid dividends continuously from 1894 through 1913, for a total of 49.25 MF, which facilitated its resort to the capital market on fairly favorable terms. Several millions more went to members of the board of directors. Thomson-Houston's ties with the Comptoir National d'Escompte were close, at first through Emile Mercet who was chairman of Thomson-Houston's board and a member of the board of the Comptoir National d'Escompte. In 1902, Mercet stepped down to become the chairman of the Comptoir National d'Escompte. Thomson-Houston is an example of a company with huge capital requirements to which retained earnings made only a small contribution. In this respect Thomson-Houston was not alone. The main subsidiaries of the Empain group in France and the Paris Metro met by 1913, respectively, only 16% and 5.5% of their capital expenditures from retained earnings.[32]

A similar reliance upon the capital market is to be found in another large electrical enterprise, the Compagnie Générale d'Electricité (CGE), which specialized in the construction of electric generating plants.[33] Founded in 1898 with the merger of four firms, three that manufactured electrical equipment and a fourth that produced electricity for the city of Rouen, the company was initially capitalized at 10 MF. It raised its capital by stages to 25 MF (nominal) by 1913:

Date	Increase	Issue Price	Yield
1900	5 MF	625	6.25 MF
1909	3 MF	710	4.26 MF
1913	7 MF		14.55 MF
TOTAL			25.06 MF

Three bond issues totaled 30 MF (nominal, the actual yield being somewhat less as the issue price varied from 468.5 to 495 francs for a 500 francs

32 M. Lévy-Leboyer, "Le système électrique en France," p. 94.
33 AN 65AQ, G160, Compagnie Generale d'Electricité.

bond): The first in 1898 for 5 MF, the second, 1899-1901, for 10 MF, and the third, 1903-1909, for 15 MF.

Like Thomson-Houston, CGE took stock in the companies of its clients. Its portfolio of shares amounted to 41.5 MF on 30 June 1913, a figure just under the totals raised by CGE on the capital market. Except for one year, 1901-1902 (1 July–30 June), when the company was hit by the depression of 1901 — losses on its portfolio of shares and the abrupt fall of the value of 1,600 tons of copper in its inventory, reduced net profits by about 75% — CGE paid regular dividends until 1913-1914. The company passed on its dividend in 1913-1914 because of uncertainties caused by the war. Total dividends paid to shareholders came to 14 MF, with an additional 1 MF going to the company's directors.

The company built up substantial reserves: 26.6 MF by 30 June 1913. The premiums on the issue of stock in 1909 and 1913 (over 8.5 MF) were added to the company's supplementary reserve. This cautious policy contributed to a relatively low dividend pay-out. New profits, including premiums on the issue of new stock, amounted to 44.6 MF for period 1 July 1898 to 30 June 1913, of which 68% were retained. It had close ties with banks as indicated by the presence of Charles Herbaut and Walter Boveri on its board.[34]

One of the six companies formed to supply electricity to the city of Paris, the Cie. Electrique Rive Gauche de Paris, offers an example of a company which generated little profit, paid few dividends, yet successfully called upon the capital market for its financial needs.[35] Founded in 1893 under the patronage of Schneider et Cie., and capitalized at 3 MF, the company raised its capital every year from 1896 through 1899 (by 1 MF each year in 1896, 1897, and 1898, and by 3 MF in 1899.) It issued bonds for 10 MF (1894-1897), 2 MF (1899), 1 MF (1901) and 6 MF (1914). Some of these securities were probably absorbed by suppliers. The nominal value of its security issues came to 25 MF (6 MF in new stock shares and 19 MF in bonds). The company paid dividends of 25 francs a share (5%) each year for its first three years of operation (presumably from capital) and 12 francs (3%) in 1900. Sharcholders, angry over the lack of dividends, precipitated the resignation of the board of directors in 1901 and in 1904. These revolts failed because the company's obligations under the concession from the city of Paris and its large bonded debt precluded the payment of dividends. The Paris municipal council combined the company's concession with that of the other five companies in 1907 and granted it to the Cie. Parisienne de Distribution d'Electricité, to take effect in 1914. In anticipation of winding up the company, profits were devoted to reducing the bonded debt. All but 1.2 MF of the bonded debt was retired by the end of 1910, when another

[34] M. Lévy-Leboyer, "Le système électrique en France," p. 95.
[35] AN 65AQ, G427, Compagnie Electrique, Rive Gauche de Paris.

stockholder's revolt brought in a new board, which rather than wind up the company, opted, using the company's generation plant at Issy-les-Moulineaux as a base, to provide electricity to the southern and western suburbs of Paris. The building of new transmission lines for this service was the reason for the new 6 MF bond issue in 1914. Lack of profits left the company little choice but to seek needed funds from suppliers and the capital market.

Like electric companies, gas companies also required large amounts of capital. A large and successful gas company, which continued to be prosperous even after the advent of electricity was the Compagnie Centrale d'Eclairage par le Gaz, Le Bon et Cie., organized as a CPA with Charles Le Bon as *gérant* in 1847 and capitalized at 1.2 MF.[36] At the outset, the company supplied gas to four communities but expanded rapidly in France, and also into Spain, Algeria and Egypt. By 1890 it possessed 37 producing units. In spite of plans to turn the company into an SARL in 1867 and stockholder sentiment, fueled by declining dividends, to transform the company into an SA in the early 1870s, it remained a CPA in the hands of the Le Bon family.

By stages, during the Second Empire, the company raised its capital to 10 MF and to 17.5 MF by 1905. A partisan of financing through the capital market, the company issued bonds totaling almost 98 MF between 1869 and 1903. Continuous dividends were paid from 1848 through 1913; from 1894 through 1913, dividends were held at a constant level of 60 francs per share. The low point for dividends occurred in the early 1870s (1873: 16 francs) owing to a lack of returns on investments in Spain, which precipitated the resignation of the original *gérant* Charles Le Bon. In 1908, 1912 and 1914, the company returned an extra 10% (50 francs) to its shareholders as reimbursement on their shares.

Transport

The Compagnie Générale Française de Tramways was founded as an SA in 1875, capitalized at 10.2 MF, to operate horse drawn trolleys serving Marseille, Le Havre, and Nancy.[37] It later expanded to other cities, including Genoa (for a time) and Tunis. A bond issue of 10 MF in 1876 provided new capital. The company's early expansion, financed largely from retained earnings, may be measured by the number of horses in its inventory: 604 horses in 1876 (31 December), 998 in 1880 and 1579 in 1890. The company brought few rewards to its investors. No dividends were forthcoming until

---

[36] AN 65AQ, G130[1-3], Compagnie Centrale d'Eclairage par le Gaz, Le Bon et Cie..

[37] AN 65AQ, Q138[1-3], Compagnie Généerale Française de Tramways.

1880; between 1880 and 1893, dividends were regularly paid, but they remained in the 2 to 3% range (10 to 14 francs on 500 francs shares). A financial reorganization took place in 1894 in which the old shareholders received 2 new shares for 5 old ones, reflecting the loss of 60% of their original capital. At the same time there was an infusion of new capital with new shares being issued for 6.12 MF, the firm's capitalization remaining at 10.2 MF. The reorganization did little to improve the company's financial plight as dividends were omitted from 1893 through 1896.

The electrification of its lines, which began in the late 1890s marked a turning point in the company's financial affairs. Electrification necessitated huge new capital outlays. The company's capitalization was increased by stages to 50 MF by 1907:

Year	New Capitalization	Addition	Issue Price	Proceeds
1898	25 MF	14.8 MF	675	19.98 MF
1902	32 MF	7 MF	900	12 MF
1905	42 MF	10 MF	510	10.2 MF
1907	50 MF	8 MF	570	9.12 MF
TOTAL ADDITION TO CAPITAL		39.8 MF		51.3 MF

All the new shares of stock were issued at a premium. Bond issues took place in 1897 for 21.1 MF almost 10 MF of which was to convert the outstanding bonded indebtedness from 5% to 4%. (This represented the original 1876 issue which had been converted from 6% to 5% bonds in 1890.) Other bond issues followed in 1901 for 2.5 MF, 3 issues in 1902 totaling 7.5 MF and another in 1904 for 5 MF. From 1906 to 1911, 60 MF of new bonds were issued of which a little over 33.5 MF was to convert or reimburse outstanding debt. In 1914 another issue for 10 MF took place. Subtracting conversions, new bonds for a nominal value of 62 MF were issued between 1897 and 1914. The total amount of new capital raised by stock and bond issues for the period 1897-1914 comes to 113 MF.

As the terms of the new stock issues indicate, the financial fortunes of the company markedly improved with electrification. On 31 December 1899 the company still possessed 1,007 horses, but a year later the number had dropped to 155. Dividends were resumed in 1897 and, with the exception of 1900, were paid continuously until 1914, with a low of 20 francs (1901) and a high of 30 francs (1899, 1906-1910). Most of the electrical equipment was obtained from Thomson-Houston, which probably absorbed much of the new security issues. In 1900 four representatives from Thomson-Houston, two directors and two officers, joined the board of the Compagnie Générale Française des Tramways.

The Chargeurs Réunis, a steamship company specializing in the transport of freight and passengers between Le Harve and South America, was founded as an SA in 1872 with a capital of 8 MF.[38] The Banque Mirabaud-Paccard played a major role in the founding of the company, and bankers remained prominent among the members of the company's board of directors. The maintenance and expansion of the company's fleet of steamers required large capital outlays. The value of ships in its inventory increased from 6.35 MF in 1872 to 12.2 MF in 1881. By this date the company possessed 10 steamers averaging a little over 2,000 tons. The fleet grew to 26 vessels in 1884, to 34 in 1902, and to 27 vessels, plus 9 under construction, in 1912. The average size of steamers in 1912 was 6,000 tons.

The company increased its capital to 12.5 MF in 1883 when it absorbed the Société Postale Français de l'Atlantique in exchange for 9,000 shares. The company relied primarily upon bonds for its external financing until 1914 when it increased its capital by 6.25 MF (to a total of 18.75 MF). Since the new issue was at 560, the company netted 7 MF. This issue was to finance the inauguration of weekly departures for Argentina leaving on a fixed day of the week, instead of the then current 39 departures a year. The choice was for a stock issue because the bonded debt of the company was already large (18 MF outstanding). The company floated a 4 MF bond issue in 1881 to help pay for the construction of seven new steamers. These bonds were reimbursed by the end of 1887. Modernizing the company's fleet resulted in a large bond issue of 25 MF, issued in 3 lots between 1900 and 1903. Although the company resorted to the capital market for extraordinary expenses, most of its financial needs were met by retained earnings. In many years the company paid high dividends, though dividends were omitted for four years: 1883-1884 (1 July–30 June), 1903-1904, and the two year period 1907-1909. Dividends were 50 francs or more for 16 years, between 25 and 50 francs for another 16 years, and between 12.5 and 25 francs for 6 years.

Housing

The burgeoning of large urban centers in the 19th century created many opportunities for companies to provide housing and other facilities for the growing population. A wave of promotion began in the late 1870s and continued until the crash of 1882 for companies devoted to buying land, building, and selling or renting.[39] By their nature these companies were predestined to use the facilities of banks, which usually sponsored their creation, of quasi-public institutions (*e.g.* the Crédit Foncier) and of the capital market for their financial needs.

---

[38] AN 65AQ, Q108[1-2], Chargeurs Réunis, Compagnie Française de Navigation à Vapeur.
[39] Michel Lescure, *Les Sociétés immobilières en France au XIXe siècle* (Paris, 1980).

The Société Foncière Lyonnaise, founded in 1879 with a capital of 50 MF (25 MF paid-in), was a creation of the Crédit Lyonnais.[40] In spite of its name, it concentrated its operations in Paris and on the Riveria. In 1880, the company raised its capital to 100 MF (50 MF paid-in); and in 1881 the company issued 12.5 MF (nominal — they were 3% bonds issued at 330 yielding 8.25 MF). Given the abundance of new issues on the market at the time, the Crédit Lyonnais experienced some difficulty in disposing of both the stocks and bonds of the Foncière. The Crash of 1882 extinguished the company's prospects. After paying dividends 1880-1883, dividends were omitted for the next ten years. In 1892, a financial reorganization took place: 125 francs was called on each of the outstanding shares of the company (total 25 MF), and then two old shares on which 375 francs had been called (250 at the time of purchase, plus the 125 francs call of 1892) were exchanged for one new share of 500 francs. This reduced the capital of the company to 50 MF; in effect, 25 MF francs of paid-in capital were written off. The following year the company issued 22 MF (nominal) of new bonds. Dividends were resumed in 1893 and paid continuously until 1914, but they were disappointingly small for investors, rising from 10 (1893) to 16.5 (1912 and 1913) francs a year.

The Société Immobilière Marseillaise fared somewhat better.[41] Founded in 1878 to build and rent small apartment buildings in Marseille, the company was initially capitalized at 10 MF. The following year it doubled its capital, issuing the new shares at a premium for an additional 1.25 MF. In 1890, the company expanded by acquiring the Nouvelle Compagnie Immobilière for stock, raising the capitalization of the company to 36.25 MF. In the same year the company issued its first bonds for 9 MF (nominal; they were 3% bonds issued at 405 for a yield of 7.29 MF), using the proceeds to pay off loans from the Crédit Foncier. A second issue followed in 1897 for 3 MF (yielding 2.76 MF). A third bond issue 3 MF was floated gradually between 1901 and 1904, and a fourth for the same amount after 1905, with almost .5 MF remaining to be issued in 1911. The company paid continuous dividends from 1879, ranging from 23 to 28.33 francs. Both the Société Foncière Lyonnaise and the Société Immobilière Marseillaise were relatively large companies in which retained earnings (net of depreciation) played a negligible role.

What these brief case studies show is that there was such diversity in corporate practice regarding retained earnings, dividend payments and issuing stocks and bonds that any meaningful generalization regarding the

---

[40] AN 65AQ, I315[1-2], Société Foncière Lyonnaise. On the founding of the company see, Jean Bouvier, *Le Crédit Lyonnais de 1863 à 1882* (2 vols.; Paris, 1961), I, pp. 476-88.

[41] AN 65AQ, I330, Société Immobilière Marseillaise.

various options is impossible. The choice of each company depended upon circumstances that varied widely. Some companies relied upon retained profits; others paid high dividends and relied upon borrowing for their capital needs; many others practiced a combination of the two. Over time, companies might shift from one policy to another. However, the evidence is such that two common generalizations — that banks declined to support domestic industry, and that French corporations were forced to rely on retained earnings — may be relegated to the dustbin. The reality was more complicated. Finally, the above examples involving the issue of securities indicates a relatively efficient French capital market.

CHAPTER V

THE CORPORATION AND INDUSTRIAL CONCENTRATION

La concurrence tue la concurrence.

P. J. Proudhon, 1846

This chapter explores various aspects of industrial concentration: The growth of large enterprises, the question of whether or not concentration was increasing, the rise of cartels, the public debate that accompanied the growth of cartels and the breakdown of legal obstacles to their spread.

The Growth of Firms

In France, and elsewhere, as the 19th century came to a close, it was obvious that large corporations were not only more numerous, but that individual corporations were growing larger, whatever the measure used: The number of employees, the amount of capital, the size of physical output, or revenues. Technological advances and expanding markets were responsible for the growth in scale, which could be achieved by employing one or more strategies: The re-investment of profits, the issue of additional stocks, or bonds, or by mergers. The term "merger" is used here to include both the uniting of two or more companies to form a new corporation, and the acquisition of one firm by another.

Although the motives for mergers are many and varied, this means of increasing firm size offers certain advantages: If achieved by the issue of new stock, it eliminated going into debt or reducing dividends. Productive capacity increases immediately, avoiding the long delays involved in the construction of new facilities. Most important in some cases, mergers could eliminate a competitor, though under other circumstances, combinations (particularly those involving vertical integration) could increase competition. Because of economies of scale, or by eliminating duplicate functions,

106

unit costs could be lowered. Financial institutions might encourage and facilitate combinations to reap underwriting profits.

In spite of the absence of adequate statistical data for mergers for the period before 1914,[1] their importance in the growth of French firms should not be underestimated.[2] Even a cursory survey of the largest industrial firms in 1914, reveals that few firms became large without absorbing other companies at one time or another. Mergers among smaller non-listed, or family-controlled, corporations are equally significant. The founding of many corporations was the result of consolidation of proprietorships and partnerships. In some sectors, mergers were more important than in others. In the iron and steel industry mergers contributed significantly to the growth of major firms. In coal mining less so, because of restrictions on combining mining concessions, but some coal mines were absorbed by iron and steel producers.

Without adequate statistical data, correlations, or lack thereof, of merger activity with general economic activity are impossible to establish. France does not appear to have experienced a merger mania at the turn of the century comparable to that which gripped the United Kingdom and the United States.[3] An increase in merger activity probably did take place in France. The rise in the number and capitalization of incorporations for the period 1898-1901 certainly reflects some increase in the number of mergers because many new corporations were products of mergers, and there is no reason to suppose that the number of mergers varies inversely with incorporations. Institutional, as well as economic reasons contributed to the presence or absence of merger waves. In the United States mergers were a way

---

[1]   Jacques Houssiaux's statistical compilation of mergers concerns primarily the period 1919-1954. Although Houssiaux does provide some figures for 1900-1914, they are, as he recognizes, incomplete. *Le pouvoir des monopoles* (Paris, 1958), pp. 337-40.

[2]   Admittedly the evidence for this statement is impressionistic, based upon upon knowledge of merger activity of several hundred corporations.

[3]   In the United States, the merger wave extended from 1898 through 1902, with 1899 the peak year when 1,208 firms disappeared, valued at more than $2.26 billion. Ralph Nelson, *Merger Movements in American Industry, 1895-1956* (Princeton, 1959), p. 37. Mergers in UK manufacturing industry peaked in 1899-1900:

Year	Number	Value (£Million)
1897	83	4.3
1898	131	8.3
1899	255	11.5
1900	244	21.9
1901	49	7.0

Leslie Hannah, *The Rise of the Corporate Economy* (Baltimore, 1976), p. 211. Hannah explains the merger wave on the basis of new technology and expanding markets, but he singles out high share prices for particular emphasis in the timing of merger waves. Ibid., pp. 22-23.

around the Sherman Act of 1890, facilitated by the jurisprudence of the Supreme Court from the Knight Case of 1895 up until the Northern Securities Decision of 1904, which contributed to the merger wave by, in effect, exempting mergers from the strictures of the Sherman Act. In France, the contemporary development of cartels, to be discussed below, served as a substitute for consolidation. Also, French courts discouraged consolidation by holding that shares of stock issued as the result of mergers were to be treated the same as shares representing non-pecuniary assets, which under the law of 1893 were non-negotiable for two years.

It was generally believed that not only were corporations growing in size but that, increasingly, one or a few giant corporations dominated the market, for sectors of industry as well as for financial services. In short, concentration, here defined as the power of a firm, or firms, over the market, was on the rise. This development was welcomed or feared according to one's lights. The appearance of such concepts as "monopoly capitalism" and "finance capitalism," the furor over "trusts," and concern for the plight of the small businessman reflect public and official recognition that concentration was the order of the day. Some were alarmed by these developments and what it signified for competition, for the survival of small firms, and what it portended for the future. Others, including both socialists and non-socialists, saw it as preparing the way for the triumph of socialism. And still others believed concentration promoted efficiency and stability. French writers constantly compared developments in Germany and the United States with those in France. The American example, in particular, was cited as something to be avoided at all costs.

In 1913, a conference on concentration was held at the Ecole des Hautes Etudes Sociales, where civil servants, scholars, and businessmen assessed the progress of concentration. Arthur Fontaine, a high official in the Ministry of Labor, observed that industrial concentration was increasing rapidly in France, noting that, according to the census of 1906, 70% of all workers were in units or factories (*établissements*) of more than 10 workers and 40% in establishments of more than 100 workers.[4] Also using the 1906 census, another participant in the conference, Lucien March, pointed out that factories employing more than 500 persons had increased to 611 in 1906 from 133 in 1840 and 441 in 1896. Factories employing more than 50 persons accounted for 49% of the French industrial workforce, which was about the same as in Germany, and also in about the same industries.[5] It should be noted that the 1906 census, being based upon individual units of

4   André Fontaine et al., *La Concentration des entreprises industrielles et commerciales* (Paris, 1913), "Introduction," pp. 21-22.
5   Lucien March, "La Concentration dans les industries de fabrication d'entretien," in Fontaine, et al., *La Concentration des entreprises industrielles et commerciales*, pp. 38ff.

production (*e.g.*, factories), rather than upon juridicial units of enterprise (*e.g.*, corporations), understates the growth of firm size. Many companies, for example Saint Gobain, which possessed 22 factories and mines in France in 1905, had more than one unit of production.

Lucien March, a partisan of concentration, argued that concentration resulted in lower prices, unless a monopoly was established; for workers, the result was higher wages and greater job stability.[6] He also predicted the spread of multinational enterprise. The economist, Charles Gide, also argued that the 1906 census figures proved the "law of concentration." However, in contrast to those like March, who saw further concentration as the wave of the future, Gide doubted that the trend would continue because of the existence of economic and natural limits to size. For Gide, the future belonged to co-operatives rather than to corporations.[7]

However, generalizations about growing concentration whether based upon the growth of size of producing units, or of firms, has its perils. Growth of firms may be accounted for by an increase in the size of the market; this does not automatically result in greater control over the market since other enterprises in the same sector may be growing at the same rate. Although the 1906 data is not comparable with earlier censuses, it appears that the number of small units (individual producers and those units with 2 to 10 employees) was also increasing.

Economists generally employ two methods for measuring concentration. The first, the "aggregate approach" pioneered by A. A. Berle and G. C. Means, examines whether or not the market share of the hundred or so largest industrial corporations is increasing or decreasing.[8] The second, the "disaggregated approach," looks at the market share of one or more of the largest firms in each sector. This approach has the advantage of differentiating among various sectors of the economy, though the thorny problem of defining sectors remains. The limited statistical evidence for the period before 1914 does not allow for a comprehensive use of either of these approaches. Since the unit of measure is the giant corporation or holding company, both of these approaches, which were designed primarily for the American economy, neglect other forms of concentration, such as cartels, the founding of filials, joint-ventures, the sharing of board members and the purchase of shares (*participations*) in other firms.

---

[6] Ibid., p. 69. March was the director of the Statistique générale de la France.

[7] Charles Gide, *Cours d'économie politique* 3rd ed. (Paris, 1913), pp. 192 fn1, 194, 223-24.

[8] A. A. Berle and G. C. Means, *The Modern Corporation and Private Property* (New York, 1936).

Industrial Concentration

The often kaleidoscopic nature of concentration may be illustrated by a brief look at the iron and steel industry. First, the firms grew larger. The average capitalization of the ten largest firms in the iron and steel industry grew from 5.8 MF in 1845 to 19.4 MF in 1869[9] and reached approximately 37 MF by 1912.[10] The degree of concentration increased rapidly during the Second Empire as firms integrated vertically to assure themselves of reliable supplies of raw materials by acquiring coal and iron ore mines. The ten largest firms accounted for about 14% of the total value of production around 1840,[11] at the beginning of the railroad age when charcoal smelting operations were still numerous. By the end of the Second Empire the share of the ten largest reached about 55% (1869),[12] and increased to 70.5% in 1912,[13] spurred in part by the high cost of new technology. This high level was temporary as the return of Alsacian firms to France following the First World War diluted concentration. In 1936 the ten largest accounted for only 57.4% of total production. In 1952 the level of concentration remained about the same as it had been at the end of the Second Empire.[14] It is also noteworthy that membership in the ten largest changed over the years. Among the ten largest firms in 1845, only six remained in 1869 and two in 1912.[15] Only four firms from 1869 were still among the top ten in 1912.[16] The iron and steel industry exhibits what may be characterized as only a moderate degree of concentration. Since the share of the largest firm did not exceed 12%, the level of concentration in the industry, of itself, suggests no threat of market domination.

---

[9] Bertrand Gille, *La Sidérurgie française au XIXe siècle* (Geneva, 1968), pp. 166 and 189.

[10] This estimate, following Gille's method, is based on nominal capital plus long-term borrowing. The average would be larger if reserves and holdings of shares in other firms (*participations*) were included, and even larger if the market value of the firm's shares were used. *E.g.*, the nominal capital, plus borrowing of Nord-Est amounted to 30 MF, not including a premium of 6 MF from a stock issue in 1906; the market value of the company was approximately 60 MF.

[11] B. Gille, *La Sidérugie française*, p. 164.

[12] Ibid., p. 189.

[13] Ibid., p. 199. Gille based his 1912 estimate on Houssiaux, who used assets, rather than market share, for his calculations.

[14] Ibid., pp. 190-91, 199-200; Jacques Houssiaux, *Le Pouvoir des monopoles* (Paris, 1958), pp. 298-307.

[15] Actually three, if the de Wendel firm is included. Although de Wendel's main branch was incorporated into the German Empire in 1871, the subsequent founding of Joeuf in French Lorraine would qualify de Wendel for inclusion in the top ten of 1912. However, the Houssiaux-Gille list for 1912 only includes listed corporations and the de Wendel firm was not a corporation.

[16] Five if de Wendel were included.

Coal mining, like the iron and steel industry, exhibited a moderate degree of concentration in 1914, based upon the output of the largest companies. It was less in 1914 than in 1850 when Gille calculated that the ten largest firms accounted for 71% of total production.[17] In part, concentration declined because of government policy: Within a few years after mid-century, the government moved to diminish this concentration by forcing the breakup of the gigantic Loire Mining Company into four separate companies. To prevent future combinations, the decree of 23 October 1852 prohibited the merger of mining concessions without government approval, but it did not prevent the acquisition of coal mines by metallurgical companies. By 1914, the Northern basin (Nord and Pas de Calais Departments) replaced the Loire as the dominant producing area, accounting for 61% of total coal production in 1913. Within this region nine companies were responsible for 80% of total production (1908-1912)[18] but on a national basis, concentration, based upon the output of the largest firms, had been greater in 1850.

The manufacture of locomotives offers another example of the viccissitudes of concentration. From 1831 to 1861, there were seventeen enterprises which manufactured locomotives, but by the 1860s the ranks were reduced to six. Two of these companies responsible for approximately one-third of French production were Alsacian, and incorporated into the German Empire in 1871. But, two new producers appeared on the scene in the 1880s, raising the number once more to six where it remained for the next thirty years. However in 1911-1912, seven new manufacturers appeared, some of which already produced rolling stock, raising the number to thirteen.[19]

Not only did concentration display wide variations between different sectors, but it could change over time and in either direction, within the same sector, as the example of the iron and steel, coal mining and the manufacture of locomotives illustrate. However, alternatives existed, and as will be seen below, the creation of cartels achieved a high degree of concentration by 1914 in portions of the iron and steel industry and coal mining without the creation a few large dominant companies.

Other industries exhibited a low degree of concentration with many firms of varying sizes: Metal working, clothing, food processing (though some sub-sectors were highly concentrated, sugar refining for example, which was dominated by an oligopoly of four large refiners). The fledgling automobile and aviation industries comprised a large number of firms in 1914, exhibit-

---

[17] B. Gille, "Les plus grandes compagnies houillères françaises vers 1840," in Trenard, ed., *Charbon*, p. 161.

[18] F. Caron, in F. Braudel and E. Labrousse, eds., *Histoire économique et sociale de la France*, IV, 1, p. 260.

[19] François Crouzet, "Essor, Déclin et Renaissance de l'Industrie Française des Locomotives, 1838-1914," *Revue d'histoire économique et sociale* 55 (1977), pp. 112-210.

ing a pattern typical of many new industries that go through stages of consolidation from low to moderate to a high degree of concentration.

Only a few industries exhibited a high degree of concentration: Glass and basic chemicals, which were both dominated by Saint Gobain, a vertically integrated multinational firm with factories in Germany, Belgium, Italy, Spain and Austria.[20] Saint Gobain was the largest of the five firms which controlled the production of basic chemicals. Also, electrical equipment, and the new oil and aluminum industries were dominated by only a few firms.

Whether or not concentration increased between the end of the Second Empire and 1914 depends upon what sector, or sub-sector, one looks at. Overall, in the absence of any detailed statistical study, it is hard to escape the conclusion that, contrary to what many contemporaries believed, concentration, based upon the size and numbers of firms, increased little, if at all during this period. Nor did the level of concentration change much over the ensuing fifty years, according to two important scholarly studies. Jacques Houssiaux found that the level of concentration, based upon the gross assets of listed companies, changed little between 1912 and 1952;[21] more recently, J. J. Carré, P. Dubois and E. Malinvaud, in their classic statistical study of the French economy in the 20th century, concluded that concentration, using numbers of factory employees as the measure, remained unchanged between 1906 and 1966.[22] Why is this the case? Certainly one reason is that, in contrast to the United States and the United Kingdom, cartels provided a substitute form of concentration.

The Rise of Cartels

The depression of 1873 marked the beginning of the modern cartel movement in Europe. Although cartels existed before 1873, it was only in the four decades preceding the outbreak of the First World War that they developed into a significant force in the economy. The appearance and expansion of cartels depended upon a complex interaction of economic, political and legal forces, which varied from country to country. Falling world prices for agricultural and industrial products from 1873 to 1896 sparked a search for ways to escape the rigors of competition and maintain prices at a remunerative

[20] M. Lévy-Leboyer, "Hierarchical Structures, Rewards and Incentives in a Large Corporation: The Early Managerial Experience of Saint Gobain, 1872-1912" in Norbert Horn and Jürgen Kocka, eds., Recht und Entwicklung des Grossunternahmen in 19. und frühen 20. Jahrhundert (Gottingen, 1975), pp. 452-59.

[21] Jacques Houssaiux, Le Pouvoir des monopoles (Paris, 1958).

[22] J. J. Carré, P. Dubois, and E. Malinvaud, French Economic Growth (Stanford, 1975), p. 165. See also, Didier and Malinvaud, "La Concentration de l'industrie s'est-elle accentuée depuis [1900] le début du siècle?" Economie et statistique No. 2 (1969).

level. Tariff protection to preserve the domestic market for native producers was high on the parliamentary agenda of most industrialized countries. The growth of cartels was closely tied to tariff protection. High tariffs enabled domestic producers to enter into agreements to maintain prices at profitable levels and avoid disastrous price swings. Cartels vary, but basically they involve agreements by independent firms to maintain prices at profitable levels by one or more of the following: Price fixing, assigning production quotas to bring supply into line with demand, dividing the market among the member firms, or establishing a common agency to handle all sales. Charging high prices to domestic customers could subsidize the dumping of surplus product abroad at less than the costs of production. In turn, chaotic world prices sometimes led to the creation of international cartels. This new era in the history of modern capitalism marked a sharp break from the competitive market model enshrined in the standard textbooks on political economy.

Scholars have generally failed to recognize the importance of cartels in France before 1914. A standard work on the consolidation of business by Robert Liefmann devoted little attention to France. According to Liefmann, the main advance in French cartels occurred after World War I and even then cartels were relatively less developed in France than in Germany, Austria, and Belgium. French cartels, he concludes, were only in their infancy by 1914, "checked . . . by the law and the more individualistic tendencies of the people."[23] Recently, Winfried Baumgart in a popular history of imperialism, expresses what is probably the prevailing view: He denies that cartels existed in France before 1914.[24] He further observes that among the great industrial powers, industrial concentration was least advanced in France, where until World War I, the small family enterprise was "the typical manufacturing unit." Not only does he underestimate the degree of economic concentration in France, but his view about the size of enterprise is only true if one takes "typical" to mean "most numerous." In fact, industrial concentration in France differed little from that of Germany.[25]

---

[23] Robert Liefmann, *Cartels, Concerns and Trusts* (London, 1932), p. 40. Originally published in German in 1905, Liefmann's book went through many editions and was greatly expanded.

[24] *Imperialism, The Idea and Reality of British and French Colonial Expansion, 1880-1914* (Oxford, 1982), p. 111. The original German edition of this work was published in 1975.

[25] For example, according to one measure of industrial concentration, the portion of the work force in factories (*établissements*) employing more than 50 workers:

	1840	1882	1906	1907
France	26%		49%	
Germany		32%		49%

Source: Charles Gide, *Cours d'économie politique* (3e ed.: Paris, 1913), p. 191.

Cartels are a form of concentration, albeit only one form and, in the long run, probably a preliminary form. Although some scholars have recognized the importance of cartels before 1914,[26] and a growing number of studies explore the operation of cartels in specific industries or regions,[27] there is no satisfactory synthesis.

A major motive for cartels and other forms of concentration was to escape the effects of competition by substituting the "visible hand" for the unstable free market. The resort to cartels and alternative forms of concentration everywhere depended upon the pace of industrial development, the national legal framework, and public reaction to it. In the United States the common law and the Sherman Act of 1890 precipitated the creation of giant holding companies and consolidation by mergers into single companies to escape legal prohibitions.[28] According to Alfred Chandler:

> Without the Sherman Act and . . . judicial interpretations, the cartels of small family firms owning and operating single-function enterprises might well have continued into the twentieth century in the United States as they did in Europe.[29]

Cartels grew rapidly in Germany without governmental hindrance and, in part as a substitute for the creation of larger enterprises.[30] In France, Article 419 of the Penal Code (1810), like the Sherman Act, appeared to rule out the creation of cartels. The language of Article 419, prohibiting any interference with the natural play of market forces in determining the level of prices, posed a barrier to modern cartel arrangements. Originally aimed at eight-

---

[26] Richard F. Kuisel, *Capitalism and the State in Modern France* (Cambridge, England, 1981), pp. 20-26; and with reservations, François Caron, *Histoire économique de la France, XIXe-XXe siècles* (Paris, 1981), pp. 149-52 and "Ententes et Stratégies d'Achat dans la France su XIXe Siècle," *Revue française de gestion*, No. 70 (1988), pp. 127-33.

[27] For example, Marcel Gillet, *Les Charbonnages du Nord de la France au XIXe siècle* (Paris, 1973), pp. 220-301; Odette Hardy-Hémery, *Industries, Patronat et Ouvriers du Valenciennois Pendant le Premier XXeme Siècle*, 5 vols. (Lille, 1985), II, pp. 603-785; Michael J. Rust, *Business and Politics: The Comité des Forges and the French Steel Industry, 1896-1914* (University Microfilms: Ann Arbor, 1974), pp. 131-185; and Jean Pierre Daviet, *Un destin international, La Compagnie de Saint Gobain de 1830 à 1939* (Paris, 1988).

[28] The constituent parts of the holding company retained their identities. When the holding company failed to provide immunity from the Sherman Act, there was a resort to the giant centralized company. Alfred Chandler, *The Visible Hand: The Managerial Revolution in American Business* (Cambridge, Mass., 1977), pp. 333-34. Chandler argues that managerial reasons were even more important than legal ones in the preference for centralized companies over holding companies.

[29] Ibid., p. 375.

[30] Erich Maschke, "Outline of the History of German Cartels from 1873 to 1914," in F. Crouzet, W. H. Chaloner, and W. S. Stern, eds., *Essays in European Economic History, 1789-1914* (London, 1969), pp. 226-58. According to Maschke, salaried managers usually preferred cartels, whereas heads of great family concerns generally favored amalgamation to form one large corporation. Ibid., 244-46.

114

eenth century practices of engrossing and regrating, the article reflected general concern over grain and bread prices. However, judges and other public officials were suspicious of the free-market model, which they saw as disruptive of the social order. So the courts and the government eventually adopted a tolerant attitude toward cartels that provided market stability and used their power over prices with moderation. Yet the latent sanction of Article 419 sensitized French businessmen to the consequences of employing their power over prices without regard to possible consequences.

The Comptoir de Longwy

Many cartel arrangements, and generally the most visibly successful ones, employed the form of a common sales agency or *comptoir*, a word used to designate a cartel in France.[31] The model for most comptoirs was that of the iron producers of Longwy, organized in 1876, which endured for 44 years. The Comptoir de Longwy was not the first; a common sales agency existed among crystal manufacturers from 1831 to 1857, enabling the firms of Baccarat and Saint Louis to dominate the French market.[32] A comptoir for Eastern salt producers existed in Nancy, and there were probably others. Four Lorraine ironmasters, Joseph Labbé, Baron Oscar d'Adelsward, Théopile Ziane, and Gustave Raty founded the Comptoir de Longwy in December 1876 to market pig iron. The Comptoir listed a positive public relations effort on behalf of Lorraine pig iron as one of its objectives, since the phosphoric Lorraine iron suffered from a poor reputation. It was an iron founders' saying that a single kilo of Lorraine pig iron would ruin the fusion of a wagon load of English pig iron. Until the discovery of the Gilchrist-Thomas process (1879), the phosphoric ore of the Lorraine could not be used for making steel or wrought iron, but was well suited for castings. With the introduction of the basic method of steelmaking, Lorraine ore could be used, though the development of steelmaking in the Meurthe-et-Moselle Department was delayed until the 1890s because de Wendel refused to share its licencing rights to the process. However pig iron was shipped to the Northern and Central regions for refining.

Within a few years the Comptoir grew to comprise most of the district's producers. Production of pig iron grew rapidly in the Meurthe-et-Moselle Department between 1877 and 1893, rising from 383,000 tons to 1,216,000

---

[31] The word *entente* was also used, but *cartel* came into general use only later, probably to avoid identification with German *Kartells*.

[32] Francois Rénaud, "Le Cartel des Cristaux, 1830-1857," *Histoire des entreprises*, 5 (1960), pp. 7-20.

tons. In 1877 the Department accounted for 25% of total French production; by 1893 its share had risen to 61%.

The Comptoir, which handled sales only, was organized as a partnership, at first for short periods of from 3 to 5½ years, and in 1910 for 25 years. It marketed throughout France and the colonies all the excess pig iron produced by its members. Most firms used the larger part of their production to make finished products, but substantial amounts remained for sale through the Comptoir. In 1899 total French production amounted to 2,567,000 tons, of which 1,565,000 came from the Meurthe-et-Moselle Department. In the same year the Comptoir disposed of 454,000 tons. Thus the Comptoir accounted for over one-sixth of total French production and about 30% of the production of the Meurthe-et Moselle Department. But the Comptoir's sales comprised most of the pig iron that was available to independent French foundries and metal working establishments.[33] Members of the Comptoir were free to export any quantities they wished; in 1905 a special Comptoir d'Exportation des Fontes de Meurthe-et-Moselle was founded to market excess production abroad. The amounts exported were never large because prices received for exported pig iron failed to cover costs, but it was a way to turn excess inventory into cash.

The Comptoir assigned customers' orders to be filled by members according to their *quantum*, the share of the Comptoir's sales to which they were entitled. The fixing of the *quantums* was the subject of careful negotiations, though member firms used most of their production for finished or semi-finished products and normally marketed less than one-fifth of their total production through the Comptoir. The Comptoir faced competition from independent producers at first, but by the turn of the century it had become virtually the only supplier of pig iron to independent metallurgical firms that did not smelt their own pig iron. Members of the Comptoir prudently limited their production to a level sufficient to satisfy their own needs and to cover their share of orders. In fact, the share sold through the Comptoir was a production quota though the Comptoir's apologists refused to recognize it as such and stoutly denied that the Comptoir was a cartel in the German sense in that no firm production quotas were established.[34] This reasoning is specious in that no member would deliberately produce more than could be marketed profitably.

In 1879, four more firms joined the original four. Membership fluctuated over the years but the tendency was always upward. With the renewal of the partnership in 1899, there were eleven members, with a nominal capital of 78,000 francs, divided among members according to their *quantum*, which

---

[33] Paul de Rousiers, *Les Syndicats industriels* (nouv. ed.: Paris, 1912) p. 190.

[34] P. de Rousiers, *Les Syndicats industriels* (Paris, 1901), pp. 198-207; Francis Laur, *De l'accaparement*, IV (Paris, 1900-1907), pp. 26-27.

determined the proportion of the Comptoir's business to which they were entitled. These shares bore some relation to their productive capacity as indicated by the number of blast furnaces for each firm, though the productive capacity of these furnaces varied (See Table 5.1). The renewal of the partnership in 1905 saw the addition of four new members and the disappearance of one, the Société Métallurgique de l'Est. The Comptoir raised its capital to 140,000 francs with each firm contributing 10,000 francs, though their *quantums* remained unequal. Of the 14 firms who were members in 1905, 11 were *sociétés anonymes*, 2 were *sociétés en commandite par actions* and one, the smallest, was a partnership. Some companies (*e.g.* Chatillon-Commentry), possessed extensive operations outside of Lorraine. In 1910 the Comptoir extended its life for 25 years and expanded its membership to 20. It failed to survive its term, disappearing in 1921. From the turn of the century the Comptoir's importance declined: In 1898, the Comptoir handled over 25% of the Department's total production; by 1913, less than 11%.[35]

The prices charged by the Comptoir were set at a level to cover costs and to assure its members of a "reasonable" return on investment. Because these prices were higher than those which would have prevailed under competitive conditions, and higher than the prevailing world prices (high duties on pig iron protected the Comptoir) customers grumbled, but the Comptoir avoided serious difficulties until the boom of 1899-1900. In 1899 the demands of the founders and metal-working establishments for pig iron rose dramatically. Since the rise in demand was unforeseen, the Comptoir, which had become the dominant supplier of pig iron for independents, was unable to fill its orders. Prices rose steeply and there were complaints that some members of the Comptoir failed to fulfill their delivery contracts in 1900. The Comptoir also reduced the interest-free period for payment from 120 to 30 days, which further irritated its clientele.

Georges Villain attacked the Comptoir in a series of articles in the influential *Les Temps*,[36] while Paul de Rousiers defended the Comptoir in his book *Les Syndicats industriels de producteurs en France et à l'étranger*, which appeared in 1901. At the Société d'Economie Politique of Paris, which devoted its meeting in March 1900 to a discussion of the Comptoir, Arthur Raffalovich argued that competition, to be instituted by abolishing the tariff on pig iron, was the remedy. However, no one but ultra-liberals took this recommendation seriously.[37] In 1901, complaints against the Comptoir

[35] P. de Rousiers, "L'Organisation commerciale de la sidérurgie française," in Comite des Forges, *La Sidérurgie française 1864-1914* (Paris, 1914), pp. 512-13.

[36] Later collected into a book, *Le Fer, la houille et la métallurgie à la fin du XIXe siècle* (Paris, 1901).

[37] *Economiste français*, 17 March 1900, pp. 340-42.

Table 5.1 Members of the Comptoir de Longwy, 1899

Firm	Comptoir Capital	Furnaces	Form* (1905)	Capitalization (1905) (MF)
1. Société Métallurgique de Gorcy	4,000	2	SA	3
2. G. Raty et Cie. (Hauts-Fourneaux de Saulnes)	10,000	4	CPA	4.25
3. Sociéte Métallurgique Senelle-Maubeuge	10,000	3	SA	9
4. F. de Saintignon et Cie. (Hauts Fourneaux de Longwy et de la Sauvage)	7,000	3	CPA	4
5. Société Métallurgique d'Aubrives et Villerupt	7,000	2	SA	6.75
6. Société Lorraine Industrielle	7,000	2	SA	4
7. Hauts-Fourneaux de la Chiers	8,000	2	SA	3
8. Hauts-Fourneaux et Fonderies de Villerupt-Laval-Dieu	7,000	2	SA	4
9. Société Métallurgique de l'Est	4,000	1	–	–
10. Chatillon-Commentry et Neuves-Maisons	10,000	4	SA	18.5
11. Forges et Fonderies de Montataire	4,000	3	SA	3.8
TOTAL	78,000	28		

Added to membership in 1905

1. Pompey			SA	10
2. Société de Hauts-Fourneaux de Maxéville			P	1.5
3. Marine et Homécourt			SA	28
4. Pont à Mousson			SA	2.047

*P: Partnership

Source: Francis Laur, *De l'accaparement*, IV, pp. 163-4, 172.

reached the floor of the Chamber of Deputies, providing a rare issue that united free trade liberals and socialists. In July 1901, one customer, smarting under the sharp rise in prices, sued the Comptoir for *accaparement*, a violation of Article 419 of the Penal Code.[38]

The Comptoir was sensitive to these attacks. After the boom was over and in the face of collapsing demand, the Comptoir lowered its prices in mid-year, even for pig iron already ordered at higher prices but undelivered. As a result, it was sued in October 1901 by one of its own members, the Société des Forges de Villerupt-Laval-Dieu, which demanded to be paid the original contract price. This trial afforded a test of the legality of the Comptoir de Longwy. Did it fall under the prohibition of Article 419? In this case, argued before the Tribunal de Briey, the influential senator and former premier Jules Méline represented the Comptoir. When the decision of the court, in February 1902, upheld the Comptoir, the Société des Forges de Villerupt-Laval-Dieu appealed. In November 1902, the Court of Nancy also held for the Comptoir. The Court decided that the Comptoir was legal, had acted within its powers, and did not come under the strictures of Article 419.[39] This decision signalled to other industries that cartels could be organized without excessive worry about the rigors of enforcement of Article 419.[40]

Other Cartels

The Comptoir de Longwy served as a model for comptoirs founded in other branches of industry, particularly during the depressed years of the mid-1890s. The Comité des Forges, a trade organization covering the whole of the metallurgical industry, fostered the organization of cartels.[41] In 1892, the Comptoir des Essieux (axels) was founded, though initial negotiations dating back to 1889 broke down over the assignment of quotas.[42] The proclaimed goal of this comptoir was to raise and stabilize prices, but it was not to sell to the state. By 1901 this comptoir had 13 members.

The Comptoir des Poutrelles (steel beams), whose membership extended from the Pyrenees to the Belgian border and included all the major

[38] Edouard Dolleans, *De l'accaparement* (Paris, 1902), pp. 326-28.

[39] F. Laur, *De l'accaparement*, IV, pp. 432-52.

[40] The Société Commerciale de Carbure, a comptoir for producers of *carbure de calcium*, which replaced price fixing agreements, appeared in 1904, inspired, in part, by the judicial decision recognizing the legality of the Comptoir de Longwy. R. O. Paxton, "L'Affaire des carbures et l'abolition du délit de coalition, 1915-1926," in P. Fridensen, ed., *Cahiers du Mouvement Social*, No. 2 (1977), pp. 145-69. Paxton surveys the conflict of opinion over cartels during and after the First World War. All of the arguments advanced were pre-figured in the period before 1914.

[41] M. Rust, *Business and Politics*, pp. 165-66.

[42] Léon Mazeaud, *Les Problèmes des unions de producteurs* (Paris, 1924), p. 26.

producers, except the French branch of de Wendel at Joeuf (Meurthe-et-Moselle), was organized in 1896 as an SA. This comptoir replaced an earlier entente of Northern and Central producers dating from 1892, which fixed prices and divided the market among themselves; the Northern and Central markets were being reserved for local producers, while Paris was divided between the two groups, with both groups selling south of the Loire at the same price. This arrangement apparently proved ineffective, because the boundaries were not respected.[43] The Comptoir possessed 22 members in 1901, but dropped to 17 in 1907, leaving outside 7 producers of which de Wendel was the most important.[44] The Comptoir existed in a state of tension between two groups: The high-cost, low-volume producers who wanted high prices, and the low-cost, high-volume producers who wanted to maintain high production and were willing to accept lower prices.[45] As in the case with the Comptoir des Essieux, the chief motive was to raise prices. The Comptoir would end cut-throat competition, which was disastrous, according to Francis Laur, a former Boulangist deputy who became a prominent apologist for cartels. "Instead, . . . a level of prices in relation to the general conditions of French production can be established on the domestic market."[46] The Comptoir also undertook the sale of surplus production to foreigners. Laur argued that the creation of this and other comptoirs helped to lower unemployment.[47] The Comptoir played a major role in standardizing girders, since uniform size and quality were essential for the successful operation of the cartel.

The Comptoir des Tôles et Larges Plats (sheet and plate steel), organized in 1895, initially comprised four producers from the Nord Department. After additions and defections, there were eight members in 1897 and ten in 1907. In spite of the lack of uniformity of its products, it managed to operate successfully. Originally organized as a co-operative, it was reorganized as an SA in 1897.[48] In the years before 1914 this comptoir accounted for approximately 90% of the sheet and plate steel sold in France, about 500,000 tons per year.[49] These and other cartels controlled the largely cartelized iron and steel industry. The Comptoir des Ressorts de Carrosserie (coach springs), organized in 1896, merely formalized long standing ententes among producers.[50] The Comptoir des Aciers Thomas (1897), which enjoyed a reputa-

---

[43] J. Carlioz, *Etude sur les associations industrielles et commerciales* (Paris, 1900), pp. 10-11.

[44] F. Laur, *De l'accaparement*, IV, pp. 34-35.

[45] M. Rust, *Business and Politics*, p. 146.

[46] F. Laur, *De l'accaparement*, IV, p. 31.

[47] Ibid., pp. 29-30.

[48] Ibid., pp. 3-23.

[49] M. Rust, *Business and Politics*, p. 147.

[50] P. de Rousiers, "l'Organisation commerciale de la sidérurgie française," p. 522.

tion for secretiveness, initially brought together five large producers who sold semi-finished bar steel for manufacture into finished products.[51] The Comptoir d'Exportation des Produits Métallurgiques (1904), which exported rails, beams, and metal railroad ties, participated in the international rail cartel. This cartel exported large quantities of rails to Brazil and Argentina. There was also an unofficial domestic rail cartel, the Entente Nationale pour les Rails, whose ten members decided who would be the lowest bidder on rail orders. The only major producer outside the entente was Alais, which was located in the heart the Paris-Lyon-Mediterranean railroad line and supplied most of the line's needs.[52]

After long negotiations, the producers of welded steel tubes entered into a cartel in 1890; in 1910 seamless steel tubes were also covered by a cartel agreement. These cartels set up a common sales agency with production quotas for each firm based upon domestic demand, the productive capacity of each firm, and its geographical location.[53] According to Catherine Omnes, the historian of the industry, the role of the cartel was not "malthusian," but provided firms with the necessary financial strength and technical competence to make them competitive on the world market, Exports went mainly to the colonies, Russia and Turkey, and were more remunerative than domestic sales.[54]

The iron ore producers of the Meurthe et Moselle Department established a cartel in 1907 to sell ore outside the Department when the increase in production of the Briey basin outran local demand. By 1914 the Comptoir had seven members and made special arrangements with other producers to sell their ore.[55]

Selling was not the sole concern. The metallurgical industry boasted several purchasing cooperatives to buy power and raw materials for its members; for example, the Société Lorraine pour le Commerce de Minerais de Fer, whose members were the same as the Comptoir de Longwy, purchased iron ore.

Cartels also became important in the sugar, paper, petroleum, glass and chemical industries. Saint Gobain dominated the cartels in both the glass and chemical industries. The Comptoir des Glaces (plate glass) was first organized in 1862 between Saint Gobain and four other companies with Saint Gobain receiving 60% of the French market. This agreement, which also contained provisions on exports to foreign markets, was renegotiated

---

[51] P. de Rousiers, *Les Syndicats industriels* (1901), p. 257.

[52] F. Laur, *De l'accaparement*, IV, p. 142.

[53] Catherine Omnès, *De L'Atelier au Groupe Industriel Vallourec, 1882-1978* (Ann Arbor, 1980), pp. 75 and 79.

[54] Ibid., pp. 78-79.

[55] M. Rust, *Business and Politics*, pp. 217-22.

frequently, but remained in force until 1892. A period of instability followed until the negotiation, under the auspices of Saint Gobain, of an international convention in 1904, uniting almost all of the continental European producers. This agreement not only covered separate cartels for the domestic markets of France, Germany and Belgium-Holland, but effectively limited production to avoid catastrophic competition on the international market.[56]

Saint Gobain was a participant in 1890 in nineteen separate cartel agreements covering products in the chemical industry.[57] Some of these agreements involved foreign producers exporting to the French market. Jean-Pierre Daviet, in his history of the Saint Gobain Company, contrasts the aggressive role of the company in the national and international markets in the glass cartel with its defensive, domestically focused role in the chemical cartels.[58] Little of importance escaped the purview of cartels in the chemical industry. An anomaly among cartels was the comptoir for alkalis, comprising four producers, organized in 1894 to replace an informal agreement of 1890. In this cartel only two of the four firms remained in production, the other two became *rentiers* by selling their production quotas to the remaining producers.[59]

The coal mines of the Nord and Pas de Calais were organized in a powerful cartel operating under the innocuous name of the Office de Statistique.[60] Marcel Gillet's account of this cartel, based upon its archives, is one of the most complete accounts of any French cartel. The major inspiration for the organization of this cartel came from the cartels of rival German and Belgian producers, particularly the Rhenish-Westphalian Coal Syndicate, though the French mining companies were aware of the numerous domestic cartels that existed among their clients.[61] Organized in 1901, the economic downturn and fear of a serious depression appears to have provided the final push, though the idea had been discussed for some years, and many of the companies had been gathering periodically to fix the price of coke.[62] The cartel aimed not only to maintain prices, but hoped to increase its market share at the expense of foreign suppliers. The basis of the cartel was a

[56] For a detailed account, see Jean Pierre Daviet, *Un Destin International, La Compagnie de Saint Gobain de 1830 à 1939* (Paris, 1988), pp. 340-53.

[57] J. Daviet, *Saint Gobain*, p. 354ff.

[58] Ibid., p. 342.

[59] Henri Morsel, "Contributions à l'histoire des ententes industrielles," *Revue d'histoire économique et sociale* 54(1976), pp. 120-22. The four were: Produits chemiques d'Alais et Camargue, Saint Gobain, Electrochemie, and the Société de l'Arre. PCAC and Saint Gobain were the two who sold their production quotas.

[60] Marcel Gillet, *Les Charbonnages du Nord de la France au XIXe siècle* (Paris, 1973), pp. 227-40.

[61] Ibid., pp. 221-22.

[62] Ibid., p. 224.

simple convention, without legal standing, relying on the good faith of the participants, signed in August 1901, which reflects the caution of the participants and their desire to be able to withdraw easily. The convention was for a trial period of one year and included 14 of the 24 companies of the Nord and Pas de Calais. Abstaining were three large companies — the giant Anzin, Marles, and Bruay — and seven small companies. The members accounted for about two-thirds of the total production of the basin.[63] The success of this cartel prompted cartel agreements covering the marketing of coke and coal briquettes, as well as the formation of three separate comptoirs to sell the chemical by-products of coke-making.

Cartels, Public Opinion, and the Law

The major motive for the founding of common sales agencies and other cartel arrangements was to escape competition, which interested businessmen equated with volatile prices and market instability. The law of 22 March 1884 permitting the creation of trade organizations (*syndicats professionnels*) not only legalized labor unions but permitted employers as well to organize to promote and defend their collective interests. What was more natural than for the representatives of an industry, gathered to promote their interests, than to agree to fix prices, limit production, or divide markets either by means of an official comptoir, or an unofficial cartel arrangement? The 1884 law signaled a change in public attitude and led the courts to enforce Article 419 less rigorously. Senator Alfred Naquet recognized this tendency when he declared in a report to the Senate in 1885: "It is true that the now out-moded dispositions of Article 419 have not been invoked for some time; hence it is perhaps pointless to ask that they be abrogated or modified."[64] Two subsequent Ministers of Justice (Fallières in 1888 and Thévenet in 1889)[65] took pains to deny this assertion, and they were generally supported by legists who pointed out that Article 419 not only continued to be applied, but that no basic contradiction existed between Article 419 and the law of 1884. After the 1884 law, cartel agreements appeared in

63 Ibid., pp. 229-31.
64 *Journal officiel, Sénat, documents parlementaires*, 1885, p. 562, cited in André Amiaud, *La Règlementation de la concurrence et les accords de chefs d'industries devant la loi pénale* (Paris, 1914), p. 150.
65 *Journal officiel, Chambre, débats parlementaires*, séance du 16 fév. 1888 and 21 mars 1889, cited in J. Carlioz, *Etude sur les associations industrielles et commericales*, p. 48. Thévenet's assertion came during a debate over Secretan's attempt to corner the copper market. Thévenet argued that because Secretan's corner was a tentative that did not succeed, Article 419 did not apply. The courts agreed. *Journel officiel, Chambre, débats parlementaire*, séance du 21 mars 1889, p. 643.

larger numbers with the toleration, if not the blessing, of the courts and government officials. Cartels have been called "the children of hard times." The stagnating economy of the 1880s and 1890s afforded a propitious environment for the steady increase in their numbers, though many were certainly ephemeral.

Francis Laur, a former deputy and a knowledgeable analyst of industrial concentration, which he favored, took issue in 1905 with the German scholar Arndt that official cartels in France were in their infancy.[66] According to Laur, there were almost 100 comptoirs in France, just half the German figure but sufficient for France "to occupy the second rank in Europe from the point of view of the number and solidity of its comptoirs and of its syndicates."[67] The difficulty in assessing the number and importance of cartels is compounded given the present state of our knowledge about secret ententes. They may have been even more numerous than official comptoirs, but possessing no legal basis, they were probably more ephemeral as well. France may have been number 2, but probably not as close a second as Laur believed. Laur himself recognized that French comptoirs were weaker than German cartels, but he considered this a virtue. For Laur, French comptoirs represented "parliamentarianism," German cartels "dictatorships," while United States trusts were "monstrous organisms."[68] Laur's fear of bigness was generally shared. He recognized that concentration was a necessity and proposed that Article 419 be revised to free businessmen of the fear of criminal penalties, which would provide a formal recognition of cartel arrangements, though he failed to specify how abuses were to be policed.[69]

Laur was not alone in his belief in the benefits and inevitability of concentration. This opinion was also widely shared, and other contemporaries like Edouard Dolléans, Paul de Rousiers, and Jules Méline agreed with Laur that comptoirs represented the ideal *via media* between wasteful competition on the one hand and German cartels and giant American holding companies on the other, particularly because they assured the continued existence of independent enterprise of moderate size.[70] These apologists stressed that the comptoirs acted with moderation. Claudio Jannet, while recognizing that there were abuses, argued that market stability was worth the slightly higher

---

[66] F. Laur, *De l'accaparement*, III, p. vii.

[67] Ibid., pp. vii and 165.

[68] F. Laur, *De l'accaparement*, IV, pp. 26-27. For Laur, industrial concentration *à outrance* could lead to the triumph of socialism, which some socialists have recognized. *De l'accaparement*, I, p. 289.

[69] F. Laur, *De l'accaparement*, I, pp. 285-86.

[70] E. Dolléans, *De l'accaparement* (Paris, 1902) p. 328 and P. de Rousiers, *Les Syndicats industriels* (1912), p. 4 and passim. See J. Méline's preface to Laur, *De l'accaparement*, vol. II.

price to consumers.[71] The economist and high government official, Clément Colson, gave a more guarded approval, recognizing that a strict application of Article 419 would have deplorable consequences.[72] J. Carlioz, an engineer, who was involved in the operation of several metallurgical comptoirs, summarized the case in their favor: They permitted economies owing to a single sales organization; they saved transport costs through a judicious division of orders; they purchased raw materials in common; they aided the struggle to survive the competition of foreign imports and organized the export of surplus product; they promoted standardized products and technical progress; finally, they benefitted workers by providing stable employment.[73]

The clients of comptoirs were less sanguine about the benefits. For example, the Association Générale des Fondeurs de France protested that the prices charged by the Comptoir de Longwy were too high. This and other complaints no doubt reflected narrow self interest more than a philosophical conviction about comptoirs. If feasible, most were only too glad to advance their own interests by similar means. There were some dissenters. Georges Villain argued to the Société d'Economie Politique of Paris, and in a series of articles in *Les Temps* that German cartels and French comptoirs were dangerous infringements on the free market.[74] For Arthur Raffalovich, the remedy was free trade, but such a radical position commanded little support except in port cities and among the regulars of the Société d'Economie Politique.[75]

The changing attitude toward the free market was also reflected by the courts. The free market was guaranteed not only by Article 419 of the Penal Code, forbidding combinations and maneuvers which would have an unnatural effect on prices, but by Articles 1131 and 1133 of the Civil Code, nullifying and rendering unenforceable illegal ententes, and by the law of 2-17 March 1791 on freedom of commerce. A leading case involving illegal ententes during the 1870s concerned the main producers of iodine in France, who organized themselves into the Union Française des Fabricants d'Iode to act as a common sales agency for its members.[76] The first agreement was made in 1870 and renewed thereafter. The entente of iodine producers also operated as a monopsony, designating a common purchasing agent to buy, at

---

71 "Des Syndicats entre industriels pour régler la production en France," pp. 24-25, extrait de *La Réforme sociale* (1895).

72 C. Colson, *Cours d'économie politique*, 5 vols. (Paris, 1901-1907) IV, p. 261.

73 J. Carlioz, *Etude sur les associations industrielles et commerciales*, pp. 37ff.

74 *Economiste français*, 17 March 1900, pp. 342-43. The *Temps* articles were collected into a book: *Le fer, la houille et la métallurgie* (1901).

75 *Economiste français*, 17 March 1900, p. 343.

76 *Cournerie c. Pellieux et Maze-Launay*, Sirey, 1879, 1: 198-200.

prices they set, from the soda producers of Brittany and Normandy. The litigation arose over a violation of the agreement by a member of the entente which exceeded its production quota and sold the excess. In 1879, the Court of Cassation, upholding an 1877 decision of the Court of Rennes, declared the union to be in violation of Article 419. This decision conformed to previous jurisprudence, though the most usual targets of judicial zeal to maintain the free market during the July Monarchy and the Second Empire appear to have been butchers and bakers.

The 1884 law, allowing professional trade organizations to be formed to defend their interests, was not only an important opening wedge, but an indication of legislative attitudes. Though the phrasing of Article 419, outlawing action that could "raise or lower" the price as determined by market forces, would seem to give the courts little room for discretion, the courts gradually moved to soften the application of the law to industrial combinations, the spirit of the times triumphing over the letter of the law. In 1888, the Court of Paris applied Article 419 to a Parisian mineral water syndicate, which imposed fixed prices on their suppliers, requiring that they sell to non-syndicate members at a higher price. The syndicate's claim that the law of 22 March 1884, in effect, abrogated Article 419 was not accepted by the Court.[77] However, a similar case fourteen years later involving the fixing of minimum prices by agreement of syndicates of book publishers and book sellers, was judged by the Court of Paris in 1902, not to violate Article 419.[78] A commentary on the case by the jurist J. Percerou noting the similarities with the mineral water syndicate case, argued that the court was using a distinction between "good" and "bad" ententes.[79] In 1894, the Court of Grenoble held that prices established by a "good" *entente* were "in harmony with the natural operation of supply and demand."[80]

The distinction between good and bad ententes was further elaborated in a leading case decided by the Court of Bordeaux in January 1900, involving an entente of lime producers.[81] In February 1891, four firms — two SAs and two proprietorships — formed a partnership, the Union des Chaux de Saint-Astier, to sell hydraulic lime produced by the four partners at a fixed high price, though each was free to sell its products north of the Loire. The

---

[77] *Grandjean et autres c. Heurteaux*, Sirey, 1889, 2: 49-51.

[78] *Le Goaziou c. Plihou et al.*, Dalloz, 1903, 2: 297-300.

[79] Ibid. The distinction between "good" and "bad" ententes resembles the "rule of reason" adopted by the Supreme Court in 1911 regarding restraints of trade under the Sherman Act.

[80] *Bonneton c. Société des tuileries*, Dalloz, 1895, 2: 221-2. The case involved a *comptoir de vente* established by the tile manufacturers in the Grenoble area. It was not a monopoly as other manufacturers existed in the area.

[81] *Mallebay c. Compagnie générale des Chaux de Saint-Astier, Société Dordognaise, Lestibondois et autres*. Sirey, 1901, 2: 225-32, note Levy-Ullmann; L. Mazeaud, *Les Problèmes des unions de producteurs*, p. 234 and Mazeaud, *Le Régime juridique des ententes* (Paris, 1928), p. 240.

partnership succeeded an earlier informal association comprised of five producers, based on a verbal agreement to fix prices that was judged to be in violation of Article 419 in December 1890. In 1895, the partnership was revised to include a fifth member. The Commercial Tribunal of Perigueux, in ruling that the union violated Article 419, triggered an appeal to the Court of Bordeaux, which agreed that the union was illegal, but not as a violation of Article 419, but rather as contrary to the principle of "freedom of commerce" and hence a violation of Articles 1131 and 1133 of the Civil Code. According to the commentary on the case by H. Lévy-Ullmann, this decision conformed to the criteria of "good and bad" ententes, bad in this particular case because of the attempt to stifle possible competitors and raise prices. In short, a bad entente aimed at abnormal profits. Obviously what constituted "abnormal" profits left a large latitude for judicial discretion, a discretion that was translated into a more tolerant attitude toward ententes. Businessmen were aware of the more lenient judicial attitude exhibited around the turn of the century. Eugène Secretan, who tried to corner the world copper market, was acquitted of violating Article 419 in 1890.[82] And the decision of the courts, noted above, in the case of the metallurgical Comptoir de Longwy served as a signal that one could proceed openly and with a good chance of impunity.

These developments lend support to Léon Mazeaud's judgment that "French courts have maintained [with regard to cartels] a perfect harmony between the law and social necessities."[83] Certainly, as François Caron has noted, "legal officials tended to think more and more that 'natural and free' competition might be dangerous and chaotic."[84] Where jurisprudence led, the law followed. The law of 3 December 1926 gave the sanction of statute to the distinction between good and bad ententes; only ententes harmful to the "general welfare" (*intérêt général*) were illegal, and for these the law removed criminal penalties.

Clearly, cartels had come a long way in France by 1914. Neither Article 419 of the Penal Code, nor the alleged "individualistic tendencies of the people" prevented their development. They were a form of concentration that avoided, at least temporarily, the advent of the American style giant holding company or the giant centralized corporation for which there was great public hostility. Apologists stressed that comptoirs were a better and a

---

82   Dalloz, 1893, 1: 49-61.

83   L. Mazeaud, *Le Régime juridique des ententes*, p. 239.
Professor Paul Pic concluded in a similar vein in 1902, ". . . après bien des hésitations, la jurisprudence française parait être parvenue à une adaptation assez hereuse et assez souple, aux nécessités contemporaines, d'un texte vieux d'un siècle, l'art. 419 du C[ode] Penal." "Les Syndicats ou coalitions de producteurs et la loi pénale," *Revue politique et parlementaire*, IX, 2e semestre (10 Nov. 1902), p. 176.

84   F. Caron, *An Economic History of Modern France* (New York, 1979), p. 43.

"French" solution to the exigencies of concentration. Although the French path toward concentration may have been generally satisfactory to public opinion, there were social costs to be borne in the form of higher prices, the persistence of inefficient enterprises, and slower technical progress. Most of those who pondered this subject thought it was worth the cost.

CONCLUSION

The Triumph of Corporate Capitalism in France

If, in 1867 there were those who believed that the corporation had a limited future, of necessity confined to large businesses where decisions could be made routinely, as Adam Smith would have it, by 1914 this illusion had virtually disappeared. From approximately 1,250 corporations in 1867, the number increased to more than ten times that number, invading virtually every sector of the economy from steel mills to department stores. Though proprietorships and partnerships continued to be numerous, their importance declined relative to the corporation. The corporation did not prove to be incompatible with prompt decision-making, and — belying another canon of conventional wisdom — hired professional managers proved to be at least as zealous and capable as owner managers, even though they were operating with other people's money. If the corporation was a virtual necessity for enterprises requiring a large amount of capital, it did not prove to be incompatible with the existence of family firms. Family firms persisted, many gaining a new lease on life by adopting the corporate form. But, over time, there was a natural tendency for family firms to pass under the control of professional managers, or to be absorbed by other corporations. The persistence of family-controlled corporations is owing the appearance of new ones as the older ones disappeared.

Allegations that the French bourgeoisie possessed a *mentalité* that was hostile to the corporation and other institutions of modern capitalism are not borne out. In the use of the corporation, France continued to be, as in the period before 1867, in the mainstream of capitalist development. Although France trailed Britain in the numbers and total capitalization of corporations, she led Germany and other European countries. This is not to say that the growth of corporations was greeted with universal acclaim. In France, as elsewhere, the growth of corporations raised fears over their power, worries over the threat to economic stability because of speculative booms and busts, and concern about the opportunities for fraudulent promoters. Though express government authorization was no longer required for incorporation, corporate foundation was subject to an array of formalities, regulations, disclosure rules and penalties, which were intended to prevent fraud. Since

129

the requirements of the law were not always effective in preventing speculative excesses and fraud, there were constant demands for stricter regulation of corporations. These demands for restrictions were opposed by both domestic and international pressures to allow relatively unrestricted access to the corporate form of business organization. The debate between liberalizers and restrictionists proved to be pretty much a draw as France steered a middle course.

One salient development of the period was the rapid rise of corporate banks, whose number before 1867 had been severely restricted. The rapid extension of branches of Parisian banks to the provinces effected a transformation in the banking structure. Small local banks disappeared in face of the competition from branch banks, often evoking an undeserved nostalgia. The charge that the large Parisian banks failed to support domestic industry in favor of channelling huge sums into foreign government bonds understates their positive contributions. It also overlooks the role of new regional corporate banks in providing financial services. In general, the banking system performed adequately in support of domestic industry. Claims that domestic industry was "starved for capital" and forced to rely on its own resources are equally false. The capital market appears to have performed fairly efficiently and played an effective role in providing financing for industry. Although a score of case studies may not provide conclusive evidence that the option of raising capital through the issue of stocks or bonds was available and often utilized, it should be noted that this conclusion is consistent with existing quantitative data.

Conclusions that economic concentration increased during the early Third Republic are open to question. The evolution of concentration in major industrial sectors varied widely. Although a few sectors exhibited a high degree of concentration, overall, concentration appears to have changed little since the end of the Second Empire. However, cartels, a substitute form of concentration, which afforded some of the benefits of huge monopolistic enterprises without the substance, took root and flowered.

In the last decades of the 19th century, a new era of capitalism emerged. The corporation became, second only to the state, the most powerful institution of modern society. Although contemporary observers often fail to recognize when institutions are in a terminal state of decay, a century later the era of corporate capitalism, though not unchallenged, continues with seemingly undiminished vigor.

BIBLIOGRAPHY

Archives Nationales, Paris

C 5426. Dossiers 1942-1945. (1) Responses of the Chambers of Commerce and courts concerning the Senate's bill on joint-stock companies, 1885-1886. (2) *Proces-verbaux des séances* of the Committee of the Chamber of Deputies, 1886-
C 5514. Dossiers 2525-2534. (1) *Proces-verbaux* of the Extra-parliamentary Commission of 1882 on joint-stock companies.(2) *Proces-verbaux* of the Committee of the Chamber of Deputies, 1890-
C 5612. Dossiers 3263-3269. *Proces-verbaux* of the Committee of the Chamber of Deputies on the 25 francs share, 1896
C 7450-7454 Parliamentary Investigation of the Rochette Affair
F^{12} 6833^A *Proces-verbaux* of the Extraparliamentary Commission of 1875
F^{12} 6833^B Responses of the Chambers of Commerce to the inquiry on the Senate's bill, 1885-1886
F^{12} 6834^A
F^{12} 6834^B
F^{12} 8850

65 AQ. These files contain company charters, a more or less complete run of annual reports, and clippings from the financial press.
A112 Banque Commerciale et Industrielle
A161 Banque Franco-Espagnol (A Rochette company)
A163 Banque France-Hollandaise
A256 Banque de l'Union Mobilière (A Rochette company)
A257$^{1-2}$ Banque de l'Union Parisienne
A480 Crédit Minier et Industriel (A Rochette company)
A753 Crédit du Nord
A809$^{1-4}$ Banque de Paris et des Pays-Bas
A950$^{1-4}$ Société Générale
A1275 Société Centrale des Banques de Province
B10$^{1-3}$ Aigle-Vie
B132$^{1-2}$ La Foncière
B245$^{1-3}$ La Nationale, Vie
F38$^{1-2}$ Docks et Entrepôts de Marseille
F48$^{1-2}$ Entrepôts et Magasins de Paris
G72 Gaz de Bordeaux
G73 Compagnie Générale d'Eclairage de Bordeaux
G130$^{1-3}$ Compagnie Centrale d'Eclairage par le Gaz, Le Bon et Cie.

G150 Compagnie Française d'Eclairage et de Chauffage par le gaz
G160 Compagnie Générale d'Electricité
G427 Compagnie Electrique, Rive Gauche de Paris
G601[1-3] Compagnie Française Thomson-Houston
I103[1] Société des Immeubles de France
I315[1-3] Société Foncière Lyonnaise
I330 Société Immobilière Marseillaise
K3[1-2] Fonderies et Forges d'Alais
K46[1-2] Forges de Chatillon-Commentry
K52 Forges de Commentry-Fourchambault
K66[1-2] Forges et Aciéries de Denain-Anzin
K123[1-3] Aciéries de Longwy
K135, K136[1-2] Forges et Aciéries de la Marine et Homécourt
K159[1-2] Forges Aciéries du Nord et de l'Est
K198 Fonderies, Forges et Aciéries de Saint Etienne
K210[1-2] Schneider et Cie.
L33 Mines d'Aniche
L83[1-2] Société des Mines de Carmaux
L248 Société des Mines de Lens
M82, M83 J. F. Cail; Société Française des Constructions Mécaniques
M200 Compagnie de Fives-Lille
P301[1-2] Compagnie de Saint Gobain
Q108[1-2] Chargeurs Réunis
Q138[1-3] Compagnie Générale Française de Tramways

Official Publications

Annuaire statistique de la France
Bulletin annexe au Journal officiel 1907-1911
Bulletin des annonces légales obligatoire à la charge des sociétés financières
    1912-1913, successor to *Bulletin annexe au Journal officiel*
Compte général de l'administration de la justice civile et commerciale
Journal officiel de la République française
Moniteur universel

Journals and Periodicals

Annuaire d'économie politique et de la statistique
Annuaires Desfossés, Annuaires des valeurs admises à la cote officiel de la Bourse
    de Paris 1891-1914
Annuaires Chaix, Les principales sociétés par actions 1892-1914
L'Economiste français
The Economist
Finance-Univers

Gazette des Tribunaux
Journal des économistes
La Marché financier
Le Moniteur des Assurances
Revue des deux mondes
Revue des societes
Sirey, J. B. *Recueil général des lois et des arrêts*

Books and Articles

Anon. "La Querelle de Lysis et de Testis jugee par Minos." *Journal des économistes*, 27 (1908): pp. 93-101
Allain, Jean Claude. *Joseph Caillaux, le défi victorieux, 1863-1914*. Paris, 1978
Amiaud, André. *La Réglementation de la concurrence et les accords de chefs d'industries devant la loi pénale*. Paris, 1914
Arnault, Louis. *Rapport de la Commission extra-parlementaire du 14 février 1882 à l'appui d'un projet de loi sur les sociétés, suivi de projet de loi soumis au Sénat le 6 décembre 1883*. Paris, 1884
Bailleux de Marisy, Alexis. "Moeurs financières de la France: I. Les Valeurs étrangères." *Revue des deux mondes*, 2nd per. 100 (1 July 1872): pp. 196-211
———. "Moeurs financières de la France: II. Les Sociétés de crédit." *Revue des deux mondes*, 2nd per. 102 (15 Nov. 1872): pp. 410-31
———. "Moeurs financières de la France: VI. Les Nouvelles sociétés foncières." *Revue des deux mondes*, 3rd per. 46 (15 Nov. 1881): pp. 432-52
Baldy, Edmond. *Les Banques d'affaires en France depuis 1900*. Paris, 1922
Beaud, Claude. "Schneider, de Wendel et les brevets Thomas." *Cahiers d'histoire* 9 (1975): pp. 363-78
Berle, A. A. and G. C. Means. *The Modern Corporation and Private Property*. New York, 1936
Blaise, Adolphe. (des Vosges). "Un Coté de l'histoire financière contemporaine." *Journal des économistes*, 4th ser. 16 (15 juin 1881): pp. 321-35
Boudet, Jacques, ed. *Le Monde des affaires en France de 1830 à nos jours*. Paris, 1952
Boudoulec, Sylvie. "Les Banques populaires des origines à la loi de 1917." *Revue de l'économie sociale* 5 (1985): pp. 17-24
Bourcart, Gabriel. "De la Nature et de l'étendue des pouvoirs de l'assemblée générale relativement aux modifications des statuts." In *Documents du Congrès Juridique International des Sociétés par Actions et des Coopératives*, edited by Louis Mathieu, I, 257-312. 2 vols. Louvain, 1910
Bouvier, Jean. *Le Crédit Lyonnais de 1863 à 1882*. 2 vols. Paris, 1922
———. *Le Krach de l'Union Générale*. Paris, 1960
———. "Rapports entre systèmes bancaires et entreprises industrielles dans la croissance européenne au XIXe siècle." In *L'Industrialisation en Europe au XIXe siècle*, edited by Pierre Léon et al., pp. 115-35. Paris, 1973
———. *Un Siècle de banque française*. Paris, 1973

Braudel, Fernand and Labrousse, Ernest, eds. *Histoire économique et sociale de la France*. 4 vols. Paris, 1970

Brockstedt, Jürgen. "Family Enterprise and the Rise of Large-Scale Enterprise in Germany, 1871-1914." In *Family Enterprise in the Era of Industrial Growth*, edited by Akio Okochi and Shigeaki Yasouka, pp. 237-67. Tokyo, 1984

Buhler, Rolf. *Die Roheisenkartelle in Frankreich; Ihre Entstehung, Entwicklung und Bedeutung von 1876 bis 1934*. Zurich, 1934

Cameron, Rondo. *France and the Economic Development of Europe*. Princeton, 1961

Capinol, Adrien A. *La Renaissance des banques locales*. Paris, 1921

Carré, J. J., Dubois, P. and Malinvaud, E. *French Economic Growth*. Stanford, 1975

Carlioz, J. *Etude sur les associations industrielles et commerciales*. Paris, 1900

Caron, François. "Les Commandes des compagnies de chemin de fer en France de 1850 à 1914." *Revue d'histoire de la sidérurgie* 6 (1965): pp. 137-76

———. *An Economic History of Modern France*. New York, 1979

———. "Ententes et stratégies d'achat dans la France du XIXe siècle." *Revue française de gestion* 70 (1988): pp. 127-33

———. *Histoire de l'exploitation d'un réeseau: la Compagnie du Chemin de Fer du Nord, 1846-1936*. Paris, 1973

———. *Histoire économique de la France, XIXe-XXe siècles*. Paris, 1981

———. "Recherches sur la capital des voies de communication en France au XIXe siècle." In *L'Industrialisation en Europe au XIXe siècle*, edited by Pierre Léon et al., pp. 237-61. Paris, 1973

———. "La Stratégie des investissements en France au XIXe et XXe siècles." *Revue d'histoire économique et sociale* 54 (1976): pp. 64-117.

Caubone. "La Concentration des entreprises en France de 1914 à 1919." *Revue d'economie politique* 34 (1920): pp. 479-88

Chandler, Alfred D. *The Visible Hand, The Managerial Revolution in American Business*. Cambridge, Mass., 1977

Cayez, Pierre. *Crises et croissance de l'industrie lyonnaise 1850-1900*. Paris, 1980

Charpenay, Georges. *Les Banques régionalistes*. Paris, 1939

Chirac, Auguste. *L'Agiotage de 1870 à 1884*. Paris, 1886

Chlepner, B. S. *Le Marché financier belge depuis cent ans*. Bruxelles, 1930

Claude, Henri. *Histoire, Réalité et destin d'un monopole, La Banque de Paris et des Pays-Bas et son groupe (1872-1968)*. Paris, 1969

Colin, Maurice. *Sur les mesures à prendre pour défendre l'épargne dans les sociétés par actions*. Paris, 1911

Collot, Claude. "Nancy, métropole financière de la Lorraine, 1871-1914." *Annales de l'Est*, 5th ser. 25 (1973): pp. 3-75

Colson, Clement. *Cours d'économie politique*. 5 vols. Paris, 1901-1907

Congrès international des sociétés par actions, 1889. *Compte rendu stenographique*. Paris, 1890

Congrès international des sociétés par actions, 1900. *Compte rendu stenographique*. Paris, 1900

Comité des Forges. *La Sidérurgie française 1864-1914*. Paris, 1914

Coste, Adolphe. *L'Anonymat, précurseur du socialisme*. Paris, 1892

Courcelle-Seneuil, J. G. "De la législation relative aux sociétés par actions." *Journal des économistes*, 4th ser. 11 (15 Aug. 1880): pp. 169-87

Cozic, H. *La Bourse, mise à la portée de tous.* Paris, 1885

Crisp, Olga. *Studies in the Russian Economy Before 1914.* London, 1976

Crouzet, François. "Essai de construction d'un indice annuel de la production industrielle française au XIXe siècle." *Annales: Economies, Sociétés, Civilisations* 25 (1970): pp. 56-99

————. "Essor, déclin et renaissance de l'industrie française des locomotives, 1838-1914." *Revue d'histoire économique et sociale* 55 (1977): pp. 112-210

————. "When the Railways Were Built." In *Business and the Businessman*, edited by Sheila Marriner, pp. 105-39. Liverpool, 1978

Cucheval-Clarigny, Athanase. "La Situation financière, le budget de 1882, la Banque de France et les sociétés financières." *Revue des deux mondes*, 3rd per. 46 (1 Aug. 1881): pp. 562-603

Daviet, Jean Pierre. *Un Destin international, La Compagnie de Saint Gobain de 1830 à 1939.* Paris, 1988

Deville, L. *Les Crises de la Bourse de Paris, 1870-1910.* Paris, 1911

Dolleans, Edouard. *De l'Accaparement.* Paris, 1902

Domergue, Jules. *Comment et pourquoi les affaires vont mal en France.* Paris, 1905

————. *La Révolution éeconomique.* Paris, 1890

————. *La Question des sociétés de crédit.* Bar le Duc, 1909

Favre, J. E. *Le Capital français au service de l'étramger, un cas: La Banque de Paris et des Pays-Bas et son oeuvre anti-nationale.* Paris, 1917

Fontaine, André. et al. *La Concentration des entreprises industrielles et commerciales.* Paris, 1913

de Foville, Alfred. *La Transformation des moyens de transport.* Paris, 1880

Freedeman, Charles E. "Cartels and the Law in France before 1914." *French Historical Studies* 16 (1988): pp. 462-78

————. "The Growth of the French Securities Market, 1815-1870." In *From the Ancien Régime to the Popular Front*, edited by C. K. Warner, pp. 75-92. New York, 1969

————. *Joint-Stock Enterprise in France, 1807-1867: From Privileged Company to Modern Corporation.* Chapel Hill, 1979

Garçon, E. ed., *Code Pénal Annoté.* 2 vols. Paris, 1901-1910

Gide, Charles. *Cours d'économie politique.* 3rd ed. Paris, 1913

Gille, Bertrand. *La Sidérurgie française au XIXe siècle.* Geneva, 1968

Gillet, Marcel. "L'Age du charbon et l'essor du bassin houiller du Nord et du Pas-de-Calais (XIXe-début XXe)." In *Charbon et sciences humaines*, edited by Louis Trenard, pp. 25-50. Paris, 1966

————. *Les Charbonnages du Nord de la France au XIXe siècle.* Paris, 1973

Girault, René. *Emprunts Russes et investissements français en Russie, 1887-1914.* Paris, 1973

————. "Portrait de l'homme d'affaires français vers 1914." *Revue d'histoire moderne et contemporaine* 16 (1969): pp. 329-49

Goffin, Robert. *Les Valeurs mobilières en France à la fin du XIXe siècle et au début du XXe siècle, 1873-1913.* Paris, 1967

Gompel, Robert. *De la Fusion des sociétés anonymes.* Paris, 1908

Guyot, Yves. "La Compagne contre les sociétés de crédit." *Journal des écono-mistes*, ser. 6. 24 (Nov. 1909): pp. 172-88

Hannah, Leslie. *The Rise of the Corporate Economy*. Baltimore, 1976

Hardy-Hémery, Odette. *De la Croissance à la désindustrialisation: Un siècle dans le Valenciennois*. Paris, 1914

———. *Industries, Patronat et Ouvriers du Valenciennois pendant le premier XXème siècle*. 5 vols. Lille, 1985

Hatt, Jacques. "Faut-il adopter la société à résponsabilité limitée allemande?" In *Documents du Congrès Juridique International des Sociétés par Actions et des Sociétés Coopératives, Bruxelles, 1910*, edited by Louis Mathieu, I, pp. 173-80. 2 vols. Louvain, 1910

Henri, Daniel. "Capitalisme familial et gestion industrielle au XIXe siècle." *Revue française de gestion* 70 (1988): pp. 141-50

Horn, Norbert and Kocka, Jüurgen, eds. *Recht und Entwicklung der Grossunter-nahmen in 19. und frühen 20. Jahrhundert*. Gotttingen, 1979

Houssiaux, Jacques. *Le Pouvoir des monopoles, Essai sur les structures indus-trielles du capitalisme*. Paris, 1958

Huart, Albin. *L'Organisation du Crédit en France*. Paris, 1913

Jacquand, Antoine. *Examen critique du projet de loi sur les sociétés par actions*. Paris, 1886

Jacquemard, Philippe. *Les Banques lorraines*. Paris, 1911

Jannet, Claudio. *La Capital, la spéculation et la finance au XIXe siècle*. Paris, 1892

———. "Des Syndicats entre industriels pour régler la production en France." Offprint from *La Réforme sociale*. Paris, 1895

Jolly, Jean, ed. *Dictionnaire des parmementaires français, 1889-1940*. 8 vols. Paris, 1960-77

Kaufmann, Eugene. *La Banque en France*. Paris, 1914

Kubicek, Robert V. *Economic Imperialism in Theory and Practice*. Durham, 1979

Kuisel, Richard F. *Capitalism and the State in Modern France*. Cambridge, England, 1981

Kurgan-van Hentenryck, G. *Rail, finance et politique: les entreprises Philippart, 1865-1890*. Brussels, 1982

Laferrère, Michel. "Le Rôle de la chemie dans l'industrialisation de Lyon au XIXe siècle." In *L'Industrialisation en Europe aux XIXe siècle*, edited by Pierre Léon et al., pp. 393-99. Paris, 1973

Laloux, Jacques. *Le Rôle des banques locales et regionales du Nord de la France dans le développement industriel et commercial*. Paris, 1924

Lambert-Dansette, Jean. "La Bourse des valeurs de Lille et l'essor des charbonn-ages au XIXe siècle." In *Charbon et sciences humaines*, edited by Louis Trenard, pp. 207-19. Paris, 1966

Laur, Francis. *De l'Accaparement*. 4 vols. Paris, 1900-1907

Laurent, E. *Notice sur quelque questions importantes*

Laydernier, Léon. *Souvenirs d'un banquier savoyard de 1884 à 1938*. Annecy, 1947

Lecouturier, Emile. *Traité des parts de fondateur*. 2nd ed. Paris, 1914

Lefebvre-Teillard, Anne. *La Société anonyme au XIXe siècle*. Paris, 1985

Léo. *La Gouffre des capitaux*. Paris, 1884

Léon, Pierre. "Crises et adaptations de la métallurgie alpine: l'usine d'Allevard, 1864-1914." *Cahiers d'histoire*, 8 (1963): pp. 6-36 and 141-64

———; Crouzet, François; and Gascon, Richard, eds. *L'Industrialization en Europe au XIXe siècle*. Paris, 1973

Leouzon le Duc, Claude Henri. *La Réforme des sociétés par actions*. Paris, 1910

Leroi, Albert. "Des Sociétés anonymes privées." In *Documents du Congrès Juridique International des Sociétés par Actions*, edited by Louis Mathieu, I, 152-72. 2 vols. Louvain, 1910

Leroy-Beaulieu, Paul. *L'Art de placer et gérer sa fortune*. Paris, 1906

———. *Essai sur la repartition des richesses*. 3rd ed. Paris, 1888

———. *Précis d'économie politique*. 5th ed. Paris, 1897

Lescure, Jean. "Les Aspects récents de la concentration industrielle." *Revue économique internationale* 3 (1909): pp. 256-96

Lescure, Michel. *Les Banques, l'état et le marché immobilier en France é l'époque contemporaine, 1820-1940*. Paris, 1982

———. *Les Sociétés immobilières en France au XIXe siècle*. Paris, 1980

Letailleur, Eugène. [Lysis]. *Les Capitalistes français contre la France*. Paris, 1916

———. *Contre l'oligarchie financière en France*. Paris, 1908

Lèvy, Raphaël Georges. "La diffusion de la fortune mobilière en France." Not dated, offprint from *La Réforme sociale*

——— and Siegfried, Jacques. *Du Relèvement du marché financier français*

———. [Testis]. *Le Rôle des établissements de crédit en France; la verité sur les propos de Lysis*. Paris, 1907

———. *Le Péril financier*. Paris, 1888

Lévy-Leboyer, Maurice. "La Décéleration de l'économie française dans la seconde moitié du XIXe siècle." *Revue d'histoire économique et sociale* 49 (1971): pp. 485-507

———. "Hierarchical Structure, Rewards and Incentives in a Large Corporation: The Early Managerial Experience of Saint Gobain, 1872-1912." In *Recht und Entwicklung der Grossunternahmen in 19. und frühen 20. Jahrhundert*, edited by Horn, Norbert and Kocka, Jürgen, pp. 451-72. Gottingen, 1979

———. *Le Patronat de la seconde industrialisation*. Cahier du *Mouvement social*, No. 4. Paris, 1979

———. "Le Système électrique en France, 1880-1940." *Revue français de gestion* 70 (1988): pp. 88-99

Leifmann, Robert. *Cartels, Concerns and Trusts*. London, 1932

Locke, Robert R. *Les Fonderies et Forges d'Alais à l'époque des premiers chemins de fer, 1829-1974*. Paris, 1978

Lysis, see Eugène Letailleur

McKay, John P. *Pioneers for Profit; Foreign Entrepreneurship and Russian Industrialization*. Chicago, 1970

———. *Tramways and Trolleys, The Rise of Urban Mass Transport in Europe*. Princeton, 1976

Malapert, F. "Les lois sur les sociétés par actions." *Journal des économistes*, 4th ser. 11 (15 Sept. 1880): pp. 340-55

March, Lucien. "La Concentration dans les industries de fabrication d'entretien."

In *La Concentration des entreprises industrielles et commerciales*, edited by André Fontaine et al., pp. 38-69. Paris, 1913

Marnata, Franéoise. *La Bourse et le financement des investissements*. Paris, 1973

Maschke, Erich. "Outline of the History of German Cartels from 1873 to 1914." In *Essays in European Economic History, 1789-1914*, edited by François Crouzet et al., pp. 226-58. London, 1969

Mathias, Peter and Postan, M. M. eds. *The Industrial Economies: Capital, Labour, and Enterprise* Vol. 8, Part 1 of the *Cambridge Economic History of Europe*. Cambridge, 1978

Mathieu, A. *Des Sociétés par actions à propos de l'affaire du Crédit Mobilier; Réponse aux adversaires de la loi du 24 juillet 1867*. Amiens, 1875

Mathieu, Louis, ed. *Documents du Congrès Juridique International des Sociétés par Actions et des Sociétés Coopératives*. 2 vols. Louvain, 1910

Mathieu-Bodet, Pierre. *Observations sur le projet de loi relatif à la réforme de la legislation sur les sociétés par actions*. Offprint from the *Journal des économistes* (15 May 1884)

Mazeaud, Leon. *Les Problèmes des unions de producteurs devant la loi française*. Paris, 1924

——. *Le Régime juridique des ententes industrielles en France*. Paris, 1928

Meeus, Joseph. *Défense de l'épargne*. Paris, 1913

Menzel, Adolphe. "Les Cartels." *Revue d'économie politique* 8 (1894): pp. 829-53

Meyer, Arthur. *Ce que mes yeux ont vu*. Paris, 1911

Michalet, C. A. *Les Placements des épargnants français de 1815 à nos jours*. Paris, 1968

Mill, Ann Wendy. "French Steel and Metal-Working Industries: A Contribution to Debate on Economic Development in Nineteenth Century France." *Social Science History* 9 (1985): pp. 307-38

Molinari, Gustave de. *L'Evolution économique au XIXe siècle; Theorie du progrès*. Paris, 1880

Monnin, P. A. *Guide pratique des capitaliste, du rentier et du spéculateur à la Bourse*. Paris, 1883

Moron, A. *La Verité sur les journaux financiéres à bon marché*. Nantes, 1882

Morsel, Henri. "Contributions à l'histoire des ententes industrielles, l'industrie des chlorates." *Revue d'histoire économique et sociale* 54 (1976): pp. 118-29

——. "Les Industries électrotechniques des Alpes françaises du Nord de 1869 à 1921." In *L'Industrialisation en Europe au XIXe siècle*, edited by Pierre Léon et al., pp. 557-87. Paris, 1972

Nelson, Ralph. *Merger Movements in American Industry, 1895-1956*. Princeton, 1959

Neymarck, Alfred. *Les Etablissements de crédit en France cinquante ans*. Paris, 1909

——. *Finances contemporaines*. 7 vols. Paris, 1902-11

——. *Rapport sur les réformes de la loi de 1867 sur les sociétés*. Paris, 1882

——. *Les Sociétés anonymes par actions, quelques réformes pratiques*. Paris, 1882

——. *Tempêtes et beaux temps de Bourse*. Paris, 1914

Nouel, René. *Les Sociétés par actions, la réforme*. Paris, 1911

Offer, Avner. "Empire and Social Reforms: British Overseas Investment and Domestic Politics, 1908-1914." *Historical Journal* 26 (1983): pp. 119-38

Ollivier, Emile. "De la liberté des sociétés." *Journal des économistes*, 4th ser. 18 (15 April 1882): pp. 50-59

Omnès, Catherine. *De l'Atelier au groupe industriel Vallourec, 1882-1918*. Ann Arbor, 1980

Paxton, Robert O. "L'Affaire des carbures et l'abolition du délit de coalition, 1915-1926." In Cahiers du *Mouvement social*, No. 2 (1977): *1914-1918, l'autre front*, edited by Patrick Fridensen, pp. 145-69

Payne, Peter L. "Family Enterprise in Britain: An Historical and Analytical Survey." In *Family Business in the Eve of Industrial Growth*, edited by Akio Okochi and Shigeaki Yasouka, pp. 119-38. Tokyo, 1984

Percerou, J. "De la Nature et de l'étendue des pouvoirs de l'assemblée générale, relativement aux modifications des statuts." In Louis Mathieu, ed. *Documents du Congrès Juridique Internationale des Sociétés par Actions et des Sociétés Coopératives*, I, 358-65. 2 vols. Louvain, 1910

Pic, Paul. "Les Syndicats au coalitions de producteurs et la loi pénale." *Revue politique et parlementaire* 29(1902): pp. 276-311

Plessis, Alain. "Le 'Retard françcais.' la faute à la banque? Banques locales, succurales de la Banque de France et financement de l'économie sous le Second Empire." In *Le Calitalisme français, XIXe-XXe siècle; blocages et dynamismes d'une croissance*, edited by Patrick Fridenson and André Straus, pp. 199-210. Paris, 1987

Pollard, Sidney. "Capital Exports, 1870-1914: Harmful or Beneficial?" *Economic History Review*, 2nd series, 38 (1985): pp. 489-513

Poidevin, Raymond. *Les Relations commerciales et financières entre la France et l'Allemagne de 1898 à 1914*. Paris, 1969

Prêcheur, Claude. *La Lorraine sidérurgique*. Paris, 1959

Prevost, Henri. *Les Ententes entre producteurs en France*. Charleville, 1904

Raffalovich, Arthur. *L'Abominable vénalité de la press d'après les documents des archives Russes (1889-1917)*. Paris, 1931

――――. "L'Accaparement des cuivres et l'effondrement du Comptoir d'Escompte." *L'Année économique, 1888-1889*. pp. 193-215

Ramon, Gabriel. *Histoire de la Banque de France*. Paris, 1929

Reboffel. *Les Coalitions de producteurs et l'article 419 du Code pénal*. Paris, 1924

Renaud, François. "Le Cartel des cristaux, 1830-1857." *Histoire des entreprises* 5 (1960): pp. 7-20

Richard, Jacques. *Etablissements de Crédit et banques locales, leur rôle, et leur utilité respectifs*. Poitiers, 1908

Ripert, Georges. *Aspects juridiques du capitalisme moderne*. Paris, 1946

――――. *Traité élementaire de droit commercial*. Paris, 1968

Rostand, Alexis. *Rapport de la troisième sous-commission*. Offprint. Paris, 1912

Roth le Gentil, Charles. *Le Mouvement de concentration des banques en France*. Paris, 1910

Rousiers, Paul de. *Les Grandes industries modernes*. 5 vols. Paris, 1924-1928

――――. "L'Organisation commerciale de la sidérurgie française." in Comité des Forges, *La Sidérurgie française, 1864-1914*, pp. 505-26. Paris, 1914

————. *Les Syndicats industriels de producteurs en France et à l'étranger.* Paris, 1901; 2nd ed. Paris, 1912

Rousseau, Rodolphe. "Rapport à le ministre du commerce." In *Congrès international des sociétés par actions, Paris 1900,* pp. 379-463. Paris, 1900

Rowley, Anthony. *Evolution économique de la France du milieu XIXe siècle à 1914.* Paris, 1982

Rust, Michael J. *Business and Politics in the Third Republic: The Comité des Forges and the French Steel Industry.* Ann Arbor: University Microfilms, 1974

Sauvel, Maurice. *Sociétés de crédit contre les banques locales.* Paris, 1901

Senès, V. *Les Origines des compagnies d'assurance fondées en France.* Paris, 1900

Siegfried, J. and R. G. Lévy. *Du Relèvement du marché financier français.* Paris, 1890

Teneul, Georges François. *Le Financement des entreprises en France depuis la fin du XIXe siècle à nos jours.* Paris, 1961

Testis. See Raphaël Georges Lévy

Thaller, Edmond Eugène. *De la Réforme de la loi sur les sociétés par actions.* Paris, 1886

————. "De la Réforme des sociétés par actions." *Revue politique et parlementaire* 35 (1903): pp. 82-125

————. *Traité élémentaire de droit commercial.* 7th ed. Paris, 1925

Théry, Edmond. *L'Evolution industriel et commerciale.* Paris, 1897

————. *Faits et chiffres, questions économiques d'actualité.* Paris, 1889

————. *La France économique et financière pendant le dernier quart de siècle.* Paris, 1897

————. *Les Valeurs mobilières en France.* Paris, 1897

Tilly, Richard H. "German Banking, 1850-1914: Development Assistance for the Strong." *Journal of European Economic History* 15 (1986): pp. 113-50

Trempé, Rolande. *Les Mineurs de Carmaux, 1848-1914.* 2 vols. Paris, 1971

Trenard, Louis, ed. *Charbon et sciences humaines.* Paris, 1966

Vavasseur, A. A. *Commentaire de la loi du 1er août 1893 sur les sociétés par actions.* Paris, 1894

————. *Un Projet de loi sur les sociétés.* Paris, 1876

————. *Sociétés, syndicats, associations devant la justice.* 2 vols. Paris, 1900

Vidal, Emmanuel. *L'Action de 25 francs dans les sociétés par actions français.* Paris, 1896

————. *The History and Methods of the Paris Bourse.* Washington, 1910

Villain, Georges. *Le Fer, la houille et la métallurgie a la fin du XIXe siècle.* Paris, 1901

Vouters, Henry. *Des Mésures législatives destinées à enrayer la concentration du commerce de détail.* Paris, 1910

White, Harry D. *The French International Accounts, 1880-1913.* Cambridge, Mass., 1933

X. *L'Exportation français et les établissements de crédit.* Paris, 1909

INDEX

A

Aciéries de Longwy, 89, 93-94
Actions d'apport, 49
Actions de porteurs, 5, 36, 42, 44, 51
Actions de priorité, 37, 42, 53-54
Actions privilégies, See Actions de priorité
Adelsward, Baron Oscar d', 115
Adelswards d', ironmaster family, 93
Agriculture, 20, 81
Aktiengesellschaft, 21
Allevard, metallurgical firm, 7-8, 76, 77
Anciens Etablissements Cail/SFCM, 95-96, 98
Aniche, mining company, 95
Anzin, mining company, 123
Arbel, banker, 40
Arnault, Louis, 30
Arndt, scholar, 124
Autofinancement, x, 83-84
Automobile industry, 18, 61, 74, 111
Aviation industry, 111
Aynard, Edouard, 78

B

Baccarat, crystal manufacturer, 115
Bange, Colonel de, 96
Bank of France, 41, 54, 67, 68, 74
Banks, xiv-xv, 20, 25, 29-34, 39-41, 57, 62-82, 103-105, 130. *See also Caisses d'épargnes*
Banque Adam, 70
Banque Charpenay, 74, 77
Banque de l'Union Parisienne, 62, 72, 73, 90
Banque de Paris, 40, 62
Banque de Paris et des Pays Bas, *See* Paribas
Banque Française pour le Commerce et l'Industrie, 25, 62, 72, 73, 77 (n. 56)

Banque Générale du Nord et du Pas de Calais, 70
Banque Henri Devilder et Cie., 69-70
Banque L. Dupont et Cie., 70
Banque Mirabaud-Paccard, 103
Banque Nationale de Crédit, 25
Banque Parisienne, 73 (n. 41)
Banque Privé Lyon-Marseille, 90
Banque Renauld et Cie., 25, 68-69
Banque Scalbert, 70
Baudelot, legislator, 30
Baudouin, legislator, 30
Baumgart, Winfried, 113
Belgian Société Générale, 73
Bender, Emile, 57 (n. 91)
Berle, A. A., 109
Bills, 39, 53-55, 81; 21 February 1883, amending the law of 1867, 36-38; 1889-90 Senate Bill on corporate law, 41-44, 46
Bismarck, 96
Blaise, Adolphe, 30
Bonnardel, Jean, 96
Bontoux, Eugène, 28, 30
Boucherot, Jules, 35
Boudenoot, L. C. F., 45
Bovary, Emma, 66
Boveri, Walter, 100
Bovykin, V.I., x
Bozérian, J. F. J., 30, 37
Brice, René, 39
Bridges, 96
Bruay, mining company, 123
Brugnot, A. B., 43 (n. 59)

C

Cail, J. F., 96
Caillaux, Joseph, 59, 63, 76 (n. 51), 79

141